IN DEFENSE OF
OPEN SOCIETY

ALSO BY GEORGE SOROS

GEORGE SOROS

IN DEFENSE OF OPEN SOCIETY

PublicAffairs

New York

PublicAffairs
Hachette Book Group
1290 Avenue of the Americas, New York, NY 10104
www.publicaffairsbooks.com
@Public_Affairs

Printed in the United States of America

First Edition: October 2019

Published by PublicAffairs, an imprint of Perseus Books, LLC, a subsidiary of Hachette Book
Group, Inc. The PublicAffairs name and logo is a trademark of the Hachette Book Group.

The Hachette Speakers Bureau provides a wide range of authors for speaking events.
To find out more, go to www.hachettespeakersbureau.com or call (866) 376-6591.

The publisher is not responsible for websites (or their content) that are not owned by
the publisher.

Editorial production by Christine Marra, Marrathon Production Services.
www.marrathoneditorial.org
Book design by Jane Raese
Set in 12.5-point Bembo

Library of Congress Cataloging-in-Publication Data has been applied for.

ISBN 978-1-5417-3670-2 (hardcover), ISBN 978-1-5417-3672-6 (ebook)

LSC-C

10 9 8 7 6 5 4 3 2 1

To the Open Society Foundations and their grantees,
whose achievements have exceeded my expectations

Contents

IN DEFENSE OF
OPEN SOCIETY

Introduction

I believe we are living in a revolutionary moment. As a result, practically anything is possible and fallibility reigns supreme.

I've had a lot of experience with revolutionary moments. They play an important role in my conceptual framework, where I distinguish between far-from-equilibrium and near-equilibrium situations. They also played an important role in my life and in the life of my foundation.

My experience with revolutionary moments started when Nazi Germany occupied Hungary in 1944. I was not yet fourteen years old. By some measures, it started even earlier, when I used to join my father in the swimming pool after school and he would regale me with tales of his adventures in Siberia during the Russian Revolution of 1917. If I add my father's reminiscences to my own experiences, I can claim to have a memory going back a hundred years.

Nineteen forty-four was the formative year in my life. One particular incident stands out in my mind. Adolf Eichmann's first act was to set up the Jewish Council, and as a schoolboy, I was sent there to act as a runner (Jewish children were forbidden to attend school). My first assignment was to deliver mimeographed notices to what turned out to be a list of lawyers whose names started with "A" and "B" to report to the Rabbinical Seminary with a change of clothes and food for twenty-four hours. Before delivering the notices, I went home to show them to my father, who was also a lawyer. He told me to deliver the messages but warn the recipients that if they reported, they would be deported. One lawyer told me that he had always been a law-abiding citizen and that they couldn't do him any harm. When I reported this to my father, he explained to me that in abnormal times the normal rules don't apply and people obey them at their peril. That became our mantra, and with his guidance all of us survived. He also helped many other people. That is what made 1944 a positive experience for me.

As regards the life of my Open Society Foundations, revolutionary moments were always important. I would mention the collapse of the Soviet system in the 1980s, which was the first time the foundation played a decisive role, and our role in Europe today, where we are trying to prevent the European Union from following the example of the Soviet Union.

In spite of the intellectual and emotional preparation, we are not exempt from the fallibility that rules supreme during revolutionary moments. We can react to events, but we cannot predict them. That means that we cannot have a firm strategy unless we call flexibility a strategy. I call it a tactic, and I endorse it. It allows us to study and prepare for various scenarios. In order to find something firm, we can rely only on our values and convictions. And that is what we are doing.

This book is entitled *In Defense of Open Society*, yet when I set up my foundation in 1979, it was not to defend open society but to promote it. For the next twenty-five years, repressive regimes like the Soviet Union were collapsing and open societies like the European Union were emerging. The trend turned negative only after the global financial crisis of 2008. The nadir was reached in 2016 with Brexit in Europe and the election of President Trump in the United States. I was an active participant in these events, and I had plenty to say about them. Now I see some early signs that the tide is turning again.

———

This book is a selection of my recent writings. It is divided into six chapters. The first chapter deals with the unprecedented dangers that confront open societies today. As the founder of the Open Society Foundations, I regard this as my primary concern today. The chapter contains two speeches I gave at the World Economic Forum in Davos in January 2018 and 2019. The 2018 speech deals with the dangers posed by social media platforms. In the 2019 speech, I warned the world of an even greater threat presented by the instruments of control that machine learning and artificial intelligence can put in the hands of repressive regimes. I focused on the Xi Jinping regime in China, which is the most advanced in these areas. I feel obliged to present the two speeches separately because my own thinking underwent a radical change during the intervening year.

I started formulating my conceptual framework as a student at the London School of Economics under the influence of my mentor, the Austrian philosopher Karl Popper, and I continued developing it over the course of my life. My philosophy has guided me both in making money and in spending it on making the world a better place—but it is not about money; it is about the complicated relationship between thinking and reality. I have decided to postpone the explanation of my philosophy until the last chapter because the best account is my article in the *Journal of Economic Methodology* in 2014. It was addressed to a specialized audience and it is therefore rather heavy going. I was afraid that I would lose many readers if I inflicted it on them early on. I hope somebody will write an explanation that is more accessible to the general public, but I am both too old and too busy to do it myself. I did, however, try to make it more accessible by revising and abridging the *Journal of Economic Methodology* article for this book.

I've devoted the second chapter to what I call *my political philanthropy*. I wrote my first essay on the subject in 2012, where I posed the questions: How could someone who is admittedly selfish and self-centered create a selfless foundation whose goal is to make the world a better place? And how can he pursue that goal even if the results don't satisfy him? I answered the questions very honestly. I have updated that essay for this book not only to reflect my current views but also because both the external situation and my foundation's structure and activities are very different today from what they were in 2012. Reflecting the changed conditions, some of my views have also changed.

The external situation has greatly deteriorated. As I explain in Chapter 1, an unprecedented danger has emerged in recent years. The rapid development of artificial intelligence and machine learning has produced instruments of social control that give repressive regimes an innate advantage over open societies. For dictatorships, they provide useful tools; for open societies, they pose a mortal danger. Our main task today is to find ways to counteract this built-in disadvantage.

In 2012, my foundation was still in an expansionary stage, although the external situation was deteriorating. I was still active in the financial markets, and my fund was making a lot of money. This put us in an unusual position, as if we were exempt from the law of gravity. Those days are over. I have retired from the financial markets, and financial repression has made it much more difficult for all fund managers to make money. At the same time, the demand for our support has greatly increased, and our supply of funds has not been able to keep up with it. Consequently, the law of gravity is catching up with us with exceptional force.

In considering the various problems confronting my foundations, I must mention another issue that I and my foundations need to deal with: aging. It is a continuous process, so it was also present in 2012, and I discussed it at length in my essay. But another seven years have passed since then. The first president of the foundation, Aryeh Neier, retired in 2012, and it fell to the new leadership headed by Patrick Gaspard, former US ambassador to South Africa, to thoroughly reorganize the foundation. They are making good progress.

Although I am in my ninetieth year, I am reluctant to retire because I feel I still have something to contribute, and as the founder, I can be faster and more entrepreneurial than the governing board that will succeed me. But I have less energy and endurance than I used to have. I have delegated many duties to my son Alex, who is also part of the new leadership.

The most dramatic positive change that has occurred in my foundation is the rising importance of the Central European University (CEU). I established it in 1991, but I hardly mentioned it in my 2012 essay. Since then, it has emerged as the foremost defender of academic freedom; it has also qualified as one of the one hundred best universities in the social sciences in the world. We have ambitious plans for its future. I consider this so important that I devote a whole chapter to it (Chapter 3).

When I was actively engaged in the financial markets, I wrote a lot on the subject. Contrary to the prevailing equilibrium theory based on the theory of rational expectations, I consider financial markets inherently unstable. My first book, *The Alchemy of Finance*, was published in 1987. Since then, it has become compulsory reading in business schools, but it was studiously ignored by academic economists until the crash of 2008. They dismissed it as the conceit of a successful hedge fund manager who imagines himself to be a philosopher. This judgment was so unanimous that I could not ignore it. I came to consider myself a failed philosopher. I even gave a lecture entitled "A Failed Philosopher Tries Again" in 1995.

All this changed after the crash of 2008. Economists could not ignore their failure to predict it. I had the pleasure of hearing the then governor of the Bank of England, Mervyn King, publicly acknowledge that my theory of the financial markets deserves consideration. The change of attitude among academic economists was even more gratifying. There was a widespread recognition that the prevailing paradigm had failed, and a willingness to rethink the basic assumptions emerged. This led me to become a sponsor of the Institute for New Economic Thinking (INET), whose mission is to break the monopoly that the efficient market hypothesis and rational expectations theory enjoyed in academic and official circles. I convoked a group of distinguished economists, including several Nobel Prize winners, and they responded enthusiastically. A board was formed under the chairmanship of Anatole Kaletsky. My friend and former colleague Rob Johnson became the president of INET and provides inspired leadership. INET is flourishing, but only because I am not on its governing board. I see a potential conflict between being the founder and a financial supporter of INET and the proponent of a particular theory of market dislocations.

I wrote a lot of articles in the aftermath of the crash. I passionately disagreed with Treasury Secretary Hank

Paulson's plan to bail out the banks by using a public fund called the Troubled Asset Relief Program (TARP) to take toxic assets off their balance sheets. I argued that it would be much more effective to inject the $700 billion provided by TARP into the balance sheet of the banks as equity. It would have gone a long way to resolve the financial crisis. I worked closely with the Democratic leadership in Congress to modify the TARP Act so as to allow the money to be used for recapitalizing the banks through the purchase of equity interests. That is what the UK government has done: it nationalized failing banks and eventually recovered most of the money it had invested. But my friend Larry Summers, who succeeded Hank Paulson, rejected it out of hand because, according to him, nationalizing banks amounted to socialism and would never be accepted in America. I had many other ideas I had hoped to put into practice when Barack Obama became president, including a fundamental reform of the mortgage system, but none of them were adopted. Some of the material written on this subject, one as recently as 2018, constitute Chapter 4 of the book.

The crash of 2008 led directly to the euro crisis of 2011. That got me interested in the deficiencies of the euro, and that led me to study the structural weaknesses of the European Union. My interest continued to grow as more and more deficiencies became apparent. My recent articles on this subject make up Chapter 5.

As mentioned before, Chapter 6 is devoted to the revised and abridged *Journal of Economic Methodology* article.

CHAPTER I

The Unprecedented Dangers Facing Open Societies

"IT Platforms and Xi Jinping's Social Credit System"

PART 1

Remarks delivered at the World Economic Forum
Davos, Switzerland, January 25, 2018

THE CURRENT MOMENT IN HISTORY

It has become something of an annual Davos tradition for me to give an overview of the current state of the world. This time I want to focus on a few issues that are foremost on my mind.

I find the current moment in history rather painful. Open societies are in crisis, and various forms of dictatorships and mafia states, exemplified by Vladimir Putin's Russia, are on the rise. In the United States, President Donald Trump would like to establish a mafia state, but he can't because the Constitution, other institutions, and a vibrant civil society won't allow it.

Whether we like it or not, my foundations, most of our grantees, and myself personally are fighting an uphill battle protecting the democratic achievements of the past. My foundations used to focus on the so-called developing world, but now that the open society is also endangered in the United States and Europe, we are spending more than half our budget closer to home because what is happening here is having a negative impact on the whole world.

But protecting the democratic achievements of the past is not enough; we must also safeguard the values of open society so that they will better withstand future onslaughts. Open society will always have its enemies, and each generation has to reaffirm its commitment to open society for it to survive.

The best defense is a well-prepared counterattack. The enemies of open society feel victorious, and this induces them to push their repressive efforts too far, generates resentment, and offers opportunities to push back. That is what is happening in places like Hungary today.

THE SURVIVAL OF OUR CIVILIZATION IS AT STAKE

I used to define the goals of my foundations as "defending open societies from their enemies, making governments accountable and fostering a critical mode of thinking." But the situation has deteriorated. Not only the survival of open society but also the survival of our entire civilization is at stake. The rise of leaders such as Kim Jong-un in North Korea and Donald Trump in the United States have much to do with this. Both seem willing to risk a nuclear war in order to keep themselves in power. But the root cause goes even deeper.

Mankind's ability to harness the forces of nature, both for constructive and destructive purposes, continues to grow while our ability to govern ourselves properly fluctuates, and it is now at a low ebb.

The threat of nuclear war is so horrendous that we are inclined to ignore it. But it is real. Indeed, the United States is set on a course toward nuclear war by refusing to accept that North Korea has become a nuclear power. This creates a strong incentive for North Korea to develop its nuclear capacity with all possible speed, which in turn may induce the United States to use its nuclear superiority preemptively—in effect to start a nuclear war in order to prevent nuclear war, an obviously self-contradictory strategy.

The fact bears repeating that North Korea has become a nuclear power and there is no military action that can prevent what has already happened. The only sensible strategy is to accept reality, however unpleasant it is, and to come to terms with North Korea as a nuclear power. This requires the United States to cooperate with all the interested parties, China foremost among them. Beijing holds most of the levers of power against North Korea but is reluctant to use them. If China came down on Pyongyang too hard, the regime could collapse, and China would be flooded by North Korean refugees. What is more, Beijing is reluctant to do any favors for the United States, South Korea, or Japan—against each of which it harbors a variety of grudges. Achieving cooperation will require extensive negotiations, but once it is attained, the alliance would be able to confront North Korea with both carrots and sticks. The sticks could be used to force North Korea to enter into good-faith negotiations and the carrots to reward it for verifiably suspending further development of nuclear weapons. The sooner a so-called freeze-for-freeze agreement can be reached, the more successful the policy will be. Success can be measured by the amount of time it would take for North Korea to make its nuclear arsenal fully operational. I'd like to draw your attention to two seminal reports just published by Crisis Group on the prospects of nuclear war in North Korea.

The other major threat to the survival of our civilization is climate change, which is also a growing cause of forced migration. I have dealt with the problems of migration at great length elsewhere, but I must emphasize how severe and intractable those problems are. I don't want to go into details on climate change either, because it is well known what needs to be done. We have the scientific knowledge; it is the political will that is missing, particularly in the Trump administration.

Clearly, I consider the Trump administration a danger to the world. But I regard it as a purely temporary phenomenon that will disappear in 2020, or even sooner. I give President Trump credit for motivating his core supporters brilliantly, but for every core supporter, he has created a greater number of core opponents who are equally strongly motivated. That is why I expect a Democratic landslide in 2018.

My personal goal in the United States is to help reestablish a functioning two-party system. This will require not only a landslide in 2018 but also a Democratic Party that will aim at nonpartisan redistricting, the appointment of well-qualified judges, a properly conducted census, and other measures that a functioning two-party system requires.

THE DANGERS POSED BY
SOCIAL MEDIA GIANTS

I want to spend the bulk of my remaining time on another global problem: the rise and monopolistic behavior of the giant IT platform companies. These companies have often played an innovative and liberating role. But as Facebook and Google have grown into ever-more powerful monopolies, they have become obstacles to innovation and have caused a variety of problems, of which we are only now beginning to become aware.

Companies earn their profits by exploiting their environment. Mining and oil companies exploit the physical environment; social media companies exploit the social environment. This is particularly nefarious because social media companies influence how people think and behave without them even being aware of it. This has far-reaching adverse consequences on the functioning of democracy, particularly on the integrity of elections.

The distinguishing features of internet platform companies is that they are networks and that they enjoy rising marginal returns, which accounts for their phenomenal growth. The network effect is truly unprecedented and transformative, but it is also unsustainable. It took Facebook eight and a half years to reach a billion users and half that time to reach the second billion. At this rate, Facebook will run out of people to convert in less than three years.

Facebook and Google effectively control over half of all internet advertising revenue. To maintain their dominance, they need to expand their networks and increase their share of users' attention. Currently they do this by providing users with a convenient platform. The more time users spend on the platform, the more valuable they become to the companies.

Content providers also contribute to the profitability of social media companies because they cannot avoid using the platforms and have to accept whatever terms they are offered.

The exceptional profitability of these companies is largely a function of their avoiding responsibility for—and avoiding paying for—the content on their platforms.

They claim they are merely distributing information. But the fact that they are near-monopoly distributors makes them public utilities and should subject them to more stringent regulations, aimed at preserving competition, innovation, and fair and open universal access.

The business model of social media companies is based on advertising. Their true customers are the advertisers. But gradually a new business model is emerging, one based not only on advertising but also on selling products and services directly to users. They exploit the data they control, bundle the services they offer, and use discriminatory pricing to keep for themselves more of the benefits that otherwise they would have to share with consumers. This enhances their profitability even further—but the bundling of services and discriminatory pricing undermine the efficiency of the market economy.

Social media companies deceive their users by manipulating their attention and directing it toward their own commercial purposes. They deliberately engineer addiction to the services they provide. This can be very harmful, particularly for adolescents. There is a similarity between internet platforms and gambling companies. Casinos have developed techniques to hook gamblers to the point where they gamble away all their money, even money they don't have.

Something very harmful and maybe irreversible is happening to human attention in our digital age. Not just distraction or addiction—social media companies are inducing people to give up their autonomy. The power to shape people's attention is increasingly concentrated in the hands of a few companies. It takes a real effort to assert and defend what John Stuart Mill called "the freedom of mind." There is a possibility that once it is lost, people who grow up in the digital age will have difficulty regaining it. This may have far-reaching political consequences. People without the freedom of mind can be easily manipulated. This danger looms not only in the future; it already played an important role in the 2016 US presidential elections.

But there is an even more alarming prospect on the horizon. There could be an alliance between authoritarian states and these large, data-rich IT monopolies that would bring together nascent systems of corporate surveillance with an already developed system of state-sponsored surveillance. This may well result in a web of totalitarian control the likes of which not even George Orwell could have imagined.

The countries in which such unholy marriages are likely to occur first are Russia and China. The Chinese IT companies in particular are fully equal to the American ones. They also enjoy the full support and protection of the Xi Jinping regime. The government of China is strong enough to protect its national champions, at least within its borders.

US-based IT monopolies are already tempted to compromise themselves in order to gain entrance to these vast and fast-growing markets. The dictatorial leaders in these countries may be only too happy to collaborate with them because they want to improve their methods of control over their own populations and expand their power and influence in the United States and the rest of the world.

The owners of the platform giants consider themselves the masters of the universe, but in fact they are slaves to preserving their dominant position. It is only a matter of time before the global dominance of the US IT monopolies is broken. Davos is a good place to announce that their days are numbered. Regulation and taxation will be their undoing, and EU Commissioner for Competition Margrethe Vestager will be their nemesis.

There is also a growing recognition of a connection between the dominance of the platform monopolies and the rising level of inequality. The concentration of share ownership in the hands of a few private individuals plays some role, but the peculiar position occupied by the IT giants is even more important. They have achieved monopoly power, but at the same time they are also competing against each other. They are big enough to swallow start-ups that could develop into competitors, but only the giants have the resources to invade each other's territory. They are poised to dominate the new growth areas that artificial intelligence is opening up, like driverless cars.

The impact of innovations on unemployment depends on government policies. The European Union and particularly the Nordic countries are much more farsighted in their social policies than the United States. They protect the workers, not the jobs. They are willing to pay for retraining or retiring displaced workers. This gives workers in Nordic countries a greater sense of security and makes them more supportive of technological innovations than workers in the United States.

The internet monopolies have neither the will nor the inclination to protect society against the consequences of their actions. That turns them into a menace, and it falls to the regulatory authorities to protect society against them. In the United States, the regulators are not strong enough to stand up against internet monopolies' political influence. The European Union is better situated because it doesn't have any platform giants of its own.

The European Union uses a different definition of monopoly power from the United States. US law enforcement focuses primarily on monopolies created by acquisitions, whereas EU law prohibits the abuse of monopoly power irrespective of how it is achieved. Europe has much stronger privacy and data protection laws than America. Moreover, US law has adopted a strange doctrine first proposed by Supreme Court Justice Robert Bork: it measures harm as an increase in the price paid by customers for services received—and that is almost impossible to prove when most services are provided for free. This leaves out of consideration the valuable data that platform companies collect from their users.

Commissioner Vestager is the champion of the European approach. It took the EU seven years to build a case against Google, but as a result of her success, the process has been greatly accelerated. Due to her proselytizing, the European approach has begun to affect attitudes in the United States as well.

THE RISE OF NATIONALISM

I have mentioned some of the most pressing and important problems confronting us today. In conclusion, let me point out that we are living in a revolutionary period. All of our established institutions are in a state of flux, and in these circumstances both fallibility and reflexivity are operating at full force.

I lived through similar conditions in my life, most recently some thirty years ago. That is when I set up my network of foundations in the former Soviet empire. The main difference between the two periods is that thirty years ago the dominant creed was international governance and cooperation. The European Union was the rising power, and the Soviet Union the declining one. Today, however, the motivating force is nationalism. Russia is resurgent, and the European Union is in danger of abandoning its values.

As you will recall, the previous experience didn't turn out well for the Soviet Union. The Soviet empire collapsed, and Russia has become a mafia state that has adopted a nationalist ideology. My foundations did quite well: the more advanced members of the Soviet empire joined the European Union.

Now our aim is to help save the European Union in order to radically reinvent it. The EU used to enjoy the enthusiastic support of the people of my generation, but that changed after the financial crisis of 2008. The EU lost its way because it was governed by outdated treaties and a mistaken belief in austerity policies. What had been a voluntary association of equal states was converted into a relationship between creditors and debtors, where the debtors couldn't meet their obligations and the creditors set the conditions that the debtors had to meet. That association was neither voluntary nor equal.

As a consequence, a large proportion of the current generation has come to regard the European Union as its enemy. One important country, Britain, is in the process of leaving the EU, and at least two countries, Poland and

Hungary, are ruled by governments that are adamantly opposed to the values on which the European Union is based. They are in acute conflict with various European institutions, and those institutions are trying to discipline them. In several other countries anti-European parties are on the rise. In Austria, an anti-European party is in the governing coalition, and the fate of Italy will be decided by the elections in March.

How can we prevent the European Union from abandoning its values? We need to reform it at every level: at the level of the Union itself, at the level of the member states, and at the level of the electorate. We are in a revolutionary period; everything is subject to change. The decisions made now will determine the shape of the future.

At the Union level, the main question is: What to do about the euro? Should every member state be required to eventually adopt the euro, or should the current situation be allowed to continue indefinitely? The Maastricht Treaty prescribed the first alternative, but the euro has developed some defects that the Maastricht Treaty didn't foresee and still await resolution.

Should the problems of the euro be allowed to endanger the future of the European Union? I would strongly argue against it. The fact is that the countries that don't qualify are eager to join, but those that do qualify have decided against it, with the exception of Bulgaria. In addition, I would like to see Britain remain a member of the EU or eventually rejoin it, and that couldn't happen if it meant adopting the euro.

The choice confronting the EU could be better formulated as one between a multispeed and a multitrack
approach. In a multispeed approach, member states have
to agree in advance on the ultimate outcome; in a multitrack approach, member states are free to form coalitions
of the willing to pursue particular goals on which they
agree. The multitrack approach is obviously more flexible,
but the European bureaucracy favored the multispeed approach. That is an important contributor to the rigidity of
the EU's structure.

At the level of the member states, their political parties are largely outdated. The old distinction between left
and right is overshadowed by being either pro- or anti-
European. This manifests itself differently in different
countries.

In Germany, the Siamese twin arrangement between
the Christian Democratic Union (CDU) and the Christian
Social Union (CSU) has been rendered unsustainable by
the results of the recent elections. There is another party,
the Alternative für Deutschland (AfD), that is further to
the right than the CSU in Bavaria. This has forced the
CSU to move further to the right in anticipation of next
year's local elections in Bavaria, so that the gap between
the CSU and the CDU has become too great. This has
rendered the German party system largely dysfunctional
until the CDU and CSU break up.

In Britain, the Conservatives are clearly the party of
the right and Labour the party of the left, but each party
is internally divided in its attitude toward Brexit. This

complicates the Brexit negotiations immensely and makes it extremely difficult for Britain as a country to decide and modify its position toward Europe.

Other European countries can be expected to undergo similar realignments, with the exception of France, which has already undergone its internal revolution.

At the level of the electorate, the top-down initiative started by a small group of visionaries led by Jean Monnet carried the process of integration a long way, but it has lost its momentum. Now we need a combination of the top-down approach of the European authorities with the bottom-up initiatives started by an engaged electorate. Fortunately, there are many such bottom-up initiatives; it remains to be seen how the authorities will respond to them. So far President Emmanuel Macron has shown himself most responsive. He campaigned for the French presidency on a pro-European platform, and his current strategy focuses on the elections for the European Parliament in 2019—and that requires engaging the electorate.

While I have analyzed Europe in greater detail, from a historical perspective, what happens in Asia is ultimately much more important. China is the rising power. There were many fervent believers in the open society in China who were sent to be re-educated in rural areas during Mao's Revolution. Those who survived returned to occupy positions of power in the government. So the future direction of China used to be open-ended, but no more.

The promoters of open society have reached retirement age, and Xi Jinping, who has more in common with Putin than with the so-called West, has begun to establish a new system of party patronage. I'm afraid that the outlook for the next twenty years is rather bleak. Nevertheless, it is important to embed China in institutions of global governance. This may help to avoid a world war that would destroy our entire civilization.

That leaves the local battlegrounds in Africa, the Middle East, and Central Asia. My foundations are actively engaged in all of them. We are particularly focused on Africa, where would-be dictators in Kenya, Zimbabwe, and the Democratic Republic of Congo have perpetrated electoral fraud on an unprecedented scale and citizens are literally risking their lives to resist the slide into dictatorship. Our goal is to empower local people to deal with their own problems, assist the disadvantaged, and reduce human suffering to the greatest extent possible. This will leave us plenty to do well beyond my lifetime.

PART 2

Remarks delivered at the World Economic Forum
Davos, Switzerland, January 24, 2019

XI JINPING'S CHINA
ENDANGERING OPEN SOCIETIES

I want to use my time tonight to warn the world about an unprecedented danger that's threatening the very survival of open societies.

Last year I discussed the nefarious role played by social media giants. Tonight, I want to call attention to the mortal danger facing open societies from the instruments of control that machine learning and artificial intelligence can put in the hands of repressive regimes. I'll focus on China, where Xi Jinping wants a one-party state to reign supreme.

A lot of things have happened since last year, and I've learned a lot about the shape that totalitarian control is going to take in China. All the rapidly expanding information available about a person is going to be consolidated in a centralized database to create a "social credit system." Based on that data, people will be evaluated by algorithms that will determine whether they pose a threat to the one-party state. People will then be treated accordingly.

The social credit system is not yet fully operational, but it's clear where it's heading. It will subordinate the fate of the individual to the interests of the one-party state in ways that are unprecedented in history.

I find the social credit system frightening and abhorrent. Unfortunately, some Chinese find it rather attractive because it provides information and services that aren't currently available and can also protect law-abiding citizens against enemies of the state.

China isn't the only authoritarian regime in the world, but it's undoubtedly the wealthiest, strongest, and most developed in machine learning and artificial intelligence. This makes Xi Jinping the most dangerous opponent of those who believe in the concept of open society. But Xi isn't alone. Authoritarian regimes are proliferating all over the world, and if they succeed, they will become totalitarian.

As the founder of the Open Society Foundations, I've devoted my life to fighting totalizing, extremist ideologies, which falsely claim that the ends justify the means. I believe that the desire of people for freedom can't be repressed forever. But I also recognize that open societies are profoundly endangered at present.

What I find particularly disturbing is that the instruments of control developed by artificial intelligence give an inherent advantage to authoritarian regimes over open societies. For them, instruments of control provide a useful tool; for open societies, they pose a mortal threat.

I use "open society" as shorthand for a society in which the rule of law prevails, as opposed to rule by a single individual, and where the role of the state is to protect human rights and individual freedom. In my personal view, an open society should pay special attention to those who suffer from discrimination or social exclusion and those who can't defend themselves.

By contrast, authoritarian regimes use whatever instruments of control they possess to maintain themselves in power at the expense of those whom they exploit and suppress.

How can open societies be protected if these new technologies give authoritarian regimes a built-in advantage? That's the question that preoccupies me. And it should also preoccupy all those who prefer to live in an open society.

Open societies need to regulate companies that produce instruments of control, while authoritarian regimes can declare them "national champions." That's what has enabled some Chinese state-owned companies to catch up with and even surpass the multinational giants.

This, of course, isn't the only problem that should concern us today. For instance, man-made climate change threatens the very survival of our civilization. But the structural disadvantage that confronts open societies is a problem that has preoccupied me, and I'd like to share with you my ideas on how to deal with it.

My deep concern for this issue arises out of my personal history. I was born in Hungary in 1930 and I'm Jewish. I was thirteen years old when the Nazis occupied Hungary and started deporting Jews to extermination camps.

I was very fortunate because my father understood the nature of the Nazi regime and arranged false identity papers and hiding places for all members of his family and for a number of other Jews as well. Most of us survived.

The year 1944 was the formative experience of my life. I learned at an early age how important it is what kind of political regime prevails. When the Nazi regime was replaced by Soviet occupation, I left Hungary as soon as I could and found refuge in England.

At the London School of Economics, I developed my conceptual framework under the influence of my mentor, Karl Popper. That framework proved to be unexpectedly useful when I found myself a job in the financial markets. The framework has nothing to do with finance but is based on critical thinking. This allowed me to analyze the deficiencies of the prevailing theories guiding institutional investors. I became a successful hedge fund manager and prided myself on being the best paid critic in the world.

Running a hedge fund was very stressful. When I had made more money than I needed for myself or my family, I underwent a kind of midlife crisis. Why should I kill myself to make more money? I reflected long and hard on what I really cared about, and in 1979 I set up the Open Society Fund. I defined its objectives as helping to open up closed societies, reducing the deficiencies of open societies, and promoting critical thinking.

My first efforts were directed at undermining the apartheid system in South Africa. Then I turned my attention to opening up the Soviet system. I set up a joint venture with the Hungarian Academy of Sciences, which was under Communist control but its representatives secretly sympathized with my efforts. This arrangement succeeded beyond my wildest dreams. I got hooked on what I like to call "political philanthropy." That was in 1984.

In the years that followed, I tried to replicate my success in Hungary and in other Communist countries. I did rather well in the Soviet empire, including the Soviet Union itself, but in China it was a different story.

My first effort in China looked rather promising. It involved an exchange of visits between Hungarian economists who were greatly admired in the Communist world and a team from a newly established Chinese think tank that was eager to learn from the Hungarians.

Based on that initial success, I proposed to Chen Yizi, the leader of the think tank, to replicate the Hungarian model in China. Chen obtained the support of Premier Zhao Ziyang and his reform-minded policy secretary, Bao Tong.

A joint venture called the China Fund was inaugurated in October 1986. It was an institution unlike any other in China. On paper, it had complete autonomy.

Bao Tong was its champion. But the opponents of radical reforms—who were numerous—banded together to attack him. They claimed that I was a CIA agent and asked the internal security agency to investigate. To protect himself, Zhao Ziyang replaced Chen Yizi with a high-ranking official in the external security police. The two organizations were co-equal, and they couldn't interfere in each other's affairs.

I approved this change because I was annoyed with Chen Yizi for awarding too many grants to members of his own institute and was unaware of the political infighting behind the scenes. But applicants to the China Fund soon noticed that the organization had come under the control of the political police and started to stay away. Nobody had the courage to explain to me the reason for it.

Eventually, a Chinese grantee visited me in New York and told me, at considerable risk to himself. Soon thereafter, Zhao Ziyang was removed from power, and I used that excuse to close the foundation. This happened just before the Tiananmen Square massacre in 1989, and it left a "black spot" on the record of the people associated with the foundation. They went to great lengths to clear their names, and eventually they succeeded.

In retrospect, it's clear that I made a mistake in trying to establish a foundation that operated in ways that were alien to people in China. At that time, giving a grant created a sense of mutual obligation between the donor and recipient and compelled both of them to remain loyal to each other forever.

WHAT HAPPENED SINCE LAST YEAR

So much for history. Let me now turn to the events that occurred in the last year, some of which surprised me.

When I first started going to China, I met many people in positions of power who were fervent believers in the principles of open society. In their youth they had been deported to the countryside to be re-educated, often suffering hardships far greater than mine in Hungary. But they survived, and we had much in common. We had all been on the receiving end of a dictatorship.

They were eager to learn about Karl Popper's thoughts on the open society. While they found the concept very appealing, their interpretation remained somewhat different from mine. They were familiar with Confucian tradition, but there was no tradition of voting in China. Their thinking remained hierarchical and carried a built-in respect for high office. I, however, was more egalitarian and wanted everyone to have a vote.

So I wasn't surprised when Xi Jinping ran into serious opposition at home, but I was surprised by the form it took. At last summer's leadership convocation at the seaside resort of Beidaihe, Xi Jinping was apparently taken down a peg or two. Although there was no official communique, rumor had it that the convocation disapproved of the abolition of term limits and the cult of personality that Xi had built around himself.

It's important to realize that such criticisms were only a warning to Xi about his excesses but did not reverse the lifting of the two-term limit. Moreover, "The Thought of Xi Jinping," which he promoted as his distillation of Communist theory, was elevated to the same level as the "Thought of Chairman Mao." So Xi remains the supreme leader, possibly for his lifetime. The ultimate outcome of the current political infighting remains unresolved.

I've been concentrating on China, but open societies have many more enemies, Putin's Russia foremost among them. And the most dangerous scenario is when these enemies conspire with and learn from each other on how to better oppress their people.

The question poses itself: What can we do to stop them?

The first step is to recognize the danger. That's why I'm speaking out tonight. But now comes the difficult part. Those of us who want to preserve the open society must work together and form an effective alliance. We have a task that can't be left to governments.

History has shown that even governments that want to protect individual freedom give precedence to the freedom of their own citizens over the freedom of the individual as a general principle, and they have many other interests.

My Open Society Foundations are dedicated to protecting human rights, especially for those who don't have a government defending them. When we started four decades ago, there were many governments that supported our efforts, but their ranks have thinned out. The United States and Europe were our strongest allies, but now they're preoccupied with their own problems.

Therefore, I want to focus on what I consider to be the most important question for open societies: What will happen in China?

The question can be answered only by the Chinese people. All we can do is to draw a sharp distinction between them and Xi Jinping. Since Xi has declared his hostility to open society, the Chinese people remain our main source of hope.

And there are, in fact, grounds for hope. As some China experts have explained to me, there is a Confucian tradition, according to which advisors of the emperor are expected to speak out when they strongly disagree with one of his actions or decrees, even if doing so may result in exile or execution.

This came as a great relief to me when I had been on the verge of despair. The committed defenders of open society in China—who are around my age—have mostly retired, and their places have been taken by younger people who are dependent on Xi Jinping for promotion. But a new political elite has emerged that is willing to uphold the Confucian tradition. This means that Xi will continue to have political opposition at home.

Xi presents China as a role model for other countries to emulate, but he's facing criticism not only at home but also abroad. His Belt and Road Initiative has been in operation long enough to reveal its deficiencies.

It was designed to promote the interests of China, not the interests of the recipient countries; its ambitious infrastructure projects were mainly financed by loans, not by grants, and foreign officials were often bribed to accept them. Many of these projects proved to be uneconomic.

The iconic case is in Sri Lanka. China built and financed a port in Sri Lanka that serves its strategic interests. When the port failed to attract sufficient commercial traffic to service the debt, this enabled China to take possession of the port. There are several similar cases elsewhere, and they're causing widespread resentment.

Malaysia is leading the pushback. The previous government headed by Najib Razak sold out to China, but in May 2018, Razak was voted out of office by a coalition led by Mahathir Mohamed. Mahathir immediately stopped several big infrastructure projects and is currently negotiating with China regarding how much compensation Malaysia will still have to pay.

The situation is not as clear-cut in Pakistan, which has been the largest recipient of Chinese investments. The Pakistani army is fully beholden to China, but the position of Imran Khan, who became prime minister last August, is more ambivalent. At the beginning of 2018, China and Pakistan announced grandiose plans in military cooperation. By the end of the year, Pakistan was in a deep financial crisis. But one thing became evident: China intends to use the Belt and Road Initiative for military purposes as well.

All these setbacks have forced Xi Jinping to modify his attitude toward the Belt and Road Initiative. In September, he announced that "vanity projects" will be shunned in favor of more carefully conceived initiatives, and in October, the *People's Daily* warned that projects should serve the interests of the recipient countries.

Customers are now forewarned, and several of them, ranging from Sierra Leone to Ecuador, are questioning or renegotiating projects.

Most importantly, the US government has now identified China as a "strategic rival." President Trump is notoriously unpredictable, but this decision was the result of a carefully prepared plan. Since then, the idiosyncratic behavior of Trump has been largely superseded by a China policy adopted by the agencies of the administration and overseen by the Asian affairs advisor of the National Security Council, Matt Pottinger, and others. The policy was outlined in a seminal speech by Vice President Mike Pence on October 4, 2018.

Even so, declaring China a strategic rival is too simplistic. China is an important global actor. An effective policy toward China can't be reduced to a slogan. It needs to be far more sophisticated, detailed, and practical, and it must include an American economic response to the Belt and Road Initiative. Pottinger's plan doesn't answer the question whether its ultimate goal is to level the playing field or to disengage from China altogether.

Xi Jinping fully understood the threat that the new US policy posed for his leadership. He gambled on a personal meeting with President Trump at the G20 meeting in Buenos Aires. In the meantime, the danger of a global trade war escalated, and the stock market embarked on a serious sell-off in December. This created problems for Trump, who had concentrated all his efforts on the 2018 midterm elections. When Trump and Xi met, both sides were eager for a deal. No wonder that they reached one, but it's very inconclusive: a ninety-day truce.

In the meantime, there are clear indications that a broad-based economic decline is in the making in China, and it is affecting the rest of the world. A global slowdown is the last thing the market wants to see.

The unspoken social contract in China is built on steadily rising living standards. If the decline in the Chinese economy and stock market is severe enough, this social contract may be undermined, and even the business community may turn against Xi Jinping. Such a downturn could also sound the death knell of the Belt and Road Initiative because Xi may run out of resources to continue financing so many loss-making investments.

On the question of global internet governance, there's an undeclared struggle between the West and China. China wants to dictate rules and procedures that govern the digital economy by dominating the developing world with its new platforms and technologies. This is a threat to the freedom of the internet and, indirectly, to open society itself.

Last year, I still believed that China ought to be more deeply embedded in the institutions of global governance, but since then, Xi Jinping's behavior has changed my opinion. My present view is that instead of waging a trade war with practically the whole world, the United States should focus on China. Instead of letting ZTE and Huawei off lightly, it needs to crack down on them. If these companies came to dominate the 5G market, they would present an unacceptable security risk for the rest of the world. But Xi Jinping's China has an Achilles' heel: it depends on foreign, mainly US-controlled sources, for the advanced chips and technology that both Huawei and STE use. By cutting off the supply, both of them will be put out of business. Placing Huawei on the "entity list" was a step in the right direction, but President Trump is more interested in pursuing his personal interests than the national interest. He let ZTE off the hook and put Huawei on the negotiating table in order to prevent a stock market selloff that might damage his chances of getting reelected in 2020.

To conclude, let me summarize the message I'm delivering tonight. My key point is that the combination of repressive regimes with IT monopolies endows those regimes with a built-in advantage over open societies. The instruments of control are useful tools in the hands of authoritarian regimes, but they pose a mortal threat to open societies.

China is not the only authoritarian regime in the world, but it is the wealthiest, strongest, and technologically most advanced. This makes Xi Jinping the most dangerous opponent of open societies. That's why it's so important to distinguish Xi's policies from the aspirations of the Chinese people. The social credit system, if it became operational, would give Xi total control over the people. Since Xi is the most dangerous enemy of the open society, we must pin our hopes on the Chinese people and, especially, on the business community and a political elite willing to uphold the Confucian tradition.

This doesn't mean that those of us who believe in the open society should remain passive. The reality is that we are in a cold war that threatens to turn into a hot one. However, if Xi and Trump were no longer in power, an opportunity would present itself to develop greater cooperation between the two cyber-superpowers.

It is possible to dream of something similar to the United Nations Treaty that arose out of the Second World War. This would be the appropriate ending to the current cycle of conflict between the United States and China. It would reestablish international cooperation and allow open societies to flourish. That sums up my message.

CHAPTER 2

My Political Philanthropy

"A Selfish Man with a Selfless Foundation"

I am both selfish and self-centered, and I have no qualms about acknowledging it. Yet over the past thirty years I have established a far-reaching philanthropic enterprise—the Open Society Foundations—whose annual budget used to hover around $500 million and is now climbing toward a billion. (Total expenditures from 1979 to 2018 are about $15 billion.) The activities of the Open Society Foundations extend to every part of the globe and cover such a wide range of subjects that even I am surprised by it. I am, of course, not the only one who is selfish and self-centered; most of us are. I am just more willing to admit it. There are many truly charitable people in the world, but few of them amass the wealth necessary to be a philanthropist.

I have always been leery of philanthropy. In my view, philanthropy goes against the grain; therefore, it generates a lot of hypocrisy and many paradoxes. Here are some examples: philanthropy is supposed to be devoted to the benefit of others, but philanthropists tend to be primarily concerned with their own benefit; philanthropy is supposed to help people, yet it often makes people dependent and turns them into objects of charity; applicants tell foundations what they want to hear, then they proceed to do what the applicant wants to do.

Given my critical attitude toward philanthropy, why do I devote such a large part of my wealth and energies to it? The answer is to be found partly in my personal background and history, partly in the conceptual framework that has guided me through my life, and partly in sheer happenstance.

The formative experience of my life was the German occupation of Hungary in 1944. I was Jewish and not yet fourteen years old. I could have easily perished in the Holocaust or suffered lasting psychological damage had it not been for my father, who understood the dangers and coped with them better than most others. My father had gone through a somewhat similar experience in the First World War, which prepared him for what happened in the Second.

As I like to tell the story, during the First World War my father joined the Austro-Hungarian army as a volunteer and was captured by the Russians. He was taken to Siberia as a prisoner of war. In the camp he became the editor of a handwritten literary magazine that was displayed on a plank, and it was called *The Plank*. The writers of the articles used to gather behind the plank and listen to the comments of the readers. My father brought home the handwritten pages, and I remember looking at them as a child. *The Plank* made him very popular, and he was elected the prisoners' representative. When some prisoners of war escaped from a neighboring camp, their representative was shot in retaliation. Instead of waiting for the same thing to happen in his camp, my father collected a group of prisoners and organized a break-out. They built a raft with the intention of drifting down to the ocean. But their knowledge of geography was deficient, and they did not realize that all the rivers of Siberia empty into the Arctic Ocean. When they recognized their mistake, they got off the raft and made their way back to civilization across the uninhabited Taiga. They got caught up in the lawlessness of the Russian Revolution and went through some harrowing adventures. That was *his* formative experience.

Eventually, my father made his way back to Hungary, but he came home a changed man. When he volunteered for the army, he had been an ambitious young man. As a result of his adventures in Russia, he lost his ambition and wanted nothing more from life than to enjoy it. Bringing up his two children was one of his chief joys. That made him a very good father. He also liked to help and guide other people and had a knack for striking up acquaintances with strangers. He held his own insights and judgment in high regard, but in other respects he was genuinely not a selfish or self-centered man.

When the Germans occupied Hungary on March 19, 1944, my father knew exactly what to do. He realized that these were abnormal times and that people who followed the normal rules were at risk. He arranged false identities not only for his immediate family but also for a larger circle. He charged a fee—sometimes quite an exorbitant one—to those who could afford it and helped others for free. I had never seen him work so hard before. That was his finest hour. Both his immediate family and most of those whom he advised or helped managed to survive.

The year of German occupation, 1944, was *my* formative experience. Instead of submitting to our fate, we resisted an evil force that was much stronger than we were—and we prevailed. It was an exhilarating adventure like the *Raiders of the Lost Ark*. Not only did we survive, but we managed to help others. This left a lasting mark on me and gave me an appetite for taking risk. Under my father's wise guidance, I learned how to cope with it— exploring the limits of the possible but not going beyond the limits. I positively relish confronting harsh reality, and I am drawn to tackling seemingly insoluble problems.

Helping others never lost its positive connotation for me, but for a long time I had few opportunities to practice it.

After the heady adventures of the war and immediate postwar period, life in Hungary became very drab. The country was occupied by Russian troops, and the Communist Party consolidated its rule. I wanted out, and with my father's help, I managed to get out. In September 1947, I left for England to study.

Life in London was a big letdown. Aged seventeen, with very little money and few connections, I was lonely and miserable. I managed to work my way through college, but it was not a pleasant experience. All students whose parents were residents in England were entitled to a county council stipend. I was an exception because my parents were not with me. Working one's way through college was not a well-trodden path, but that is what I had to do.

I had two encounters with philanthropy during that difficult period, and they have colored my attitude toward charity ever since. Shortly after I arrived in London, I turned to the Jewish Board of Guardians to ask for financial support. They refused me on the grounds that their guidelines called for supporting only young people who were learning a trade, not students. Later on, when I was already a student at the London School of Economics, I took on a temporary job at Christmastime as a railroad porter, and I broke my leg. I came out of the hospital on crutches, and I thought this was a good opportunity to get some money out of the Jewish Board of Guardians. I climbed two flights of stairs on my crutches and asked them for temporary support. They repeated their mantra about helping only apprentices, but they couldn't refuse me. They gave me three pounds, hardly enough to live on for a week. This continued for several weeks. Each time I had to climb the stairs on crutches to collect the money.

In the meantime, my roommate, having heard my story, decided to go to the Jewish Board of Guardians and declare himself ready to learn a trade. He didn't last long in the jobs they found for him, but they kept supporting him. After a while, they wanted to send me to the Industrial Injuries Board for assistance, but I said I could not go there because I was working illegally and did not want to endanger my student visa. That was not true. My temporary job on the railroad was perfectly legal, but they did not know that. They had sent a social worker to check on me, but he did not find out. So when they refused me further assistance, I felt morally justified to write an impassioned letter to the chairman of the board in which I said that "I will manage to survive, but it makes me sad that the board of which you are the chairman is unwilling to help a young Jewish student who had broken his leg and was in need." That had the desired effect. The chairman arranged for me to receive three pounds a week by mail without having to climb the stairs. After the crutches came off and after I took a hitchhiking holiday in the south of France, I wrote to the chairman, telling him that I no longer needed his assistance and thanked him for it. Although I had deceived the foundation, I felt morally justified because they had investigated my case and did not find out that I was lying. Under these circumstances, I considered their behavior unjust.

My next encounter with philanthropy was when I was working nights as a waiter in a nightclub while studying during the day. When my tutor found out about it, she turned to the Quakers, who sent me a questionnaire. After I filled it out, they sent me a check for forty pounds without any strings attached. That impressed me as the right way to help people. After the crash of 2008, I was able to arrange for nearly a million New York schoolchildren whose families were on welfare or food stamps to receive a check for $200, no questions asked. I put up 20 percent of the cost on behalf of New York State in order to qualify for a grant from the federal government as part of the economic stimulus package. The Quakers' generosity bore ample dividends sixty years later, and I felt good about that in spite of the vicious attacks by the *New York Post* on "welfare handouts."

After finishing college, I had a difficult time finding my way in the world. I had a number of false starts in England and eventually ended up in New York, first as an arbitrage trader, then as a security analyst and institutional salesman, and finally as the manager of one of the first hedge funds. During that period, I was not particularly philanthropic. The only venture worth mentioning was an attempt to restore Central Park. In partnership with Dick Gilder, a broker and investor, we set up the Central Park Community Fund, but it was not particularly successful. Another organization, the Central Park Conservancy, established a close working relationship with the park administration and made much greater progress in restoring the park. My greatest accomplishment was to dissolve our organization and merge it into the successful one. During the process, I discovered that charitable organizations have a life of their own that is independent of their stated mission, and it is easier to set up a charity than to wind it down.

Starting as a student at the London School of Economics and continuing in New York, I developed the theory of reflexivity, that served to guide me both in making money as a hedge fund manager and, later, in spending it as a policy-oriented philanthropist. For reasons explained in the Introduction, the latest version is available in Chapter 6.

My conceptual framework was not as well developed in my college days as it is today. But the core ideas were already there, and they extended not only to economics but also to politics and human affairs in general. My thinking was greatly influenced by Karl Popper, the Austrian-born philosopher, first through his book *Open Society and Its Enemies* and then through his theory of scientific method.

I finished my undergraduate courses a year early, and I had a year to kill before I would earn my degree. I chose Karl Popper as my tutor and wrote a couple of essays for him. After college I had to earn a living, but I never lost my interest in the complicated relationship between thinking and reality. I submitted an essay entitled "The Burden of Consciousness" to Popper several years after I left college.

My business career followed a tortuous path, with many false starts and missteps, but eventually I ended up in charge of one of the first hedge funds in New York. I started in 1969 with about $3 million. By 1979, the fund reached $100 million, mostly from retained earnings. About $40 million of that belonged to me. I considered that was more than enough for me and my family. The strain of risk taking on a leveraged basis was enormous. On one occasion, I subscribed to a very large amount of a new issue of British government bonds on short notice without previously arranging the necessary financing. I was rushing around the City of London, trying to find a credit line, and while walking down Leadenhall Street, I thought I was having a heart attack. "I took on this risk to make a killing," I told myself, "but if I die now, I end up as the loser. It doesn't make sense to risk my life to make money." That is when I decided to do something worthwhile with my money and set up a foundation. I thought long and hard about what I really cared about. I relied on my rather abstract conceptual framework for guidance, and I honed in on the concept of open society, which is one of the cornerstones of that framework.

As far as I know, the term "open society" was first used by Henri Bergson, the French philosopher, in his essay "Two Sources of Morality and Religion." One source was tribal and led to a closed society; the other was universal and was associated with an open society. Karl Popper pointed out that open societies can be turned into closed ones by universal ideologies that claim to be in possession of the ultimate truth. That claim is false; therefore, such ideologies can prevail only by using methods of compulsion. By contrast, open societies recognize that different people have different views and interests; they introduce man-made laws to enable people to live together in peace. Having experienced both Nazi and Communist rule in Hungary, I was deeply impressed by Popper's ideas. I defined the mission of my foundation as (1) opening closed societies, (2) making open societies more viable, and (3) promoting a critical mode of thinking. That was in 1979.

STARTING UP

The foundation had a slow start. I was aware of the pitfalls and paradoxes of philanthropy, and I wanted to avoid them. I undertook an apprenticeship at Helsinki Watch, a fledgling human rights organization that later became the Human Rights Watch. I attended the Wednesday morning meetings, where current events and activities were discussed. I also went on a fact-finding trip to El Salvador and Nicaragua, which were both at that time in the midst of civil war. I learned a lot but did relatively little on my own. I did get involved with a Russian refugee, Vladimir Bukovsky, who was active in Soviet-occupied Afghanistan. But I stopped supporting him when I realized that his activities could result in people killing or getting killed.

Later, I went to Russia on another fact-finding trip, and there I struck up an intimate relationship with a *refusenik* and started sending him money through a Swissair stewardess for distribution to other dissidents in Russia. Eventually, my foundation became a major source of financial support for dissident movements throughout Eastern Europe.

My first major independent undertaking was in South Africa. I had a Zulu friend in New York, Herbert Vilakazi, who was a university lecturer in Connecticut. He returned to South Africa to take up a post at the University of Transkai—one of the homelands under the apartheid system. I visited him in 1980 and gained an insight into South Africa from an unusual angle. Here was a closed society with all the institutions of a first-world country, but they were off limits to the majority of the population on racial grounds. Where could I find a better opportunity for opening up a closed society? I met with the vice chancellor of Cape Town University, Stuart Saunders, who was eager to open the university to black students. All students accepted by the university had their tuition paid by the state. I jumped at the opportunity to use the resources of the apartheid state for opening it up and offered to pay the living expenses for eighty black students.

I visited South Africa again the next year, but that trip was less successful. I wanted to support African arts and culture, so I asked Nadine Gordimer, who would go on to win a Nobel Prize for literature, to arrange a meeting with African cultural leaders to discuss how best to do it. But the meeting was a flop. By then, my cover was blown. Everyone knew that I was a wealthy philanthropist from New York, and the meeting's participants saw a pot of gold sitting in the middle of the room; all they could discuss was how to divide it up amongst themselves. I decided to abandon my project, disappointing everyone.

I also visited Cape Town University and discovered that the number of black students had increased by fewer than eighty, either because some of the Open Society scholarships were given to students already enrolled or because some students had dropped out. The students I met seemed thoroughly disaffected. They felt unwelcome, discriminated against, and forced into an alien culture, and they had difficulties meeting the academic requirements. I also met with the faculty and found them far less open-minded than the vice chancellor.

I decided to discontinue the scheme; I would, however, see the first cohort through. In retrospect, discontinuing the project turned out to be a bad decision. The vice chancellor engaged a black mentor for the black students—it happened to be my friend Herbert Vilakazi—and subsequently they did much better. It would have been great to have a larger number of black university graduates when the apartheid system was abolished. But at the time I made my decision, the apartheid system seemed firmly established. I tried a few other projects as well, but I came to feel that nothing I did would change the system. The fact that they tolerated my activities merely served to demonstrate how tolerant they were. Instead of me taking advantage of the apartheid state, the apartheid state seemed to be taking advantage of me: by tolerating my activities, they improved their image abroad. Looking back, I wish I had been more persistent. This experience taught me that it is worth fighting for seemingly hopeless causes.

My next major venture was in my native Hungary. In the early 1980s, the Communist regime in Hungary was eager to be accepted by the International Monetary Fund (IMF) and the World Bank, and this offered me an opportunity to bring out a group of Hungarian dissidents to spend a year at New York University: they were allowed to leave the country. That gave me a knowledge base about Hungary on which I could build.

In 1984, I approached the Hungarian government about setting up a foundation there, and somewhat to my surprise, they responded positively. We engaged in protracted negotiations, in which I was guided by my dissident friends. It was agreed that my foundation would support Hungarian culture in general and not only dissidents. The Hungarian Academy of Sciences, then under the strict control of the Central Committee of the Communist Party, was designated as my partner.

I visited the country repeatedly and selected a group of people in whom I could have confidence and who were also acceptable to the government. Together with the vice president of the Academy, they would constitute the board of our joint venture. So far so good. But then the authorities insisted that the decisions of the board should be carried out by a secretariat staffed by the reliable political appointees controlled by the secret police, and that was a deal breaker. I went to see the cultural czar of the Communist Party, George Aczel, to inform him that we had reached an impasse.

"I hope you won't leave with bad feelings," he said.

"I can't help it, having put so much effort into it," I answered.

I was already at the door when he said, "What would it take for you to go ahead?"

"An independent secretariat," I replied.

We agreed to have two secretaries, one nominated by the Academy and one by me. Every document would have to be countersigned by both to be valid. That is how the Hungarian foundation came into existence. I also hired my first employee, a Hungarian émigré, in New York at what eventually became the headquarters of the Open Society Foundations. Until then, the staff had consisted of my second wife, Susan Weber.

The foundation in Hungary worked like a charm. It was exempt from all the pitfalls that beset normal foundations because civil society adopted it as its own. We relied on a simple precept I derived from Karl Popper's concept of open society: the state dogma, promoted by the ruling Communists, was false; by providing any alternative to the ideological monopoly of the one-party state, we could expose its falsehood to the public. Accordingly, the foundation supported every cultural initiative that was not an expression of official dogma—from zither clubs to farmers' cooperatives. The amounts awarded were very small because most of the initiatives used facilities provided by the state and the people engaged in them drew salaries from the state. We used the state's own resources to undermine it.

The Hungarian forints needed for these awards were generated by giving dollar grants to cultural and educational institutions. They were flush with Hungarian forints but devoid of foreign currency, so they were willing to make contributions to the Hungarian foundation at much better than the official exchange rate. Our most successful venture was to provide them with Xerox machines. This served a dual purpose: not only did it secure Hungarian currency for the Hungarian foundation, but it also spread information that was not otherwise easily available. The Leadership Institute of the Karl Marx University of Economics and the Philosophy Institute of the Hungarian Academy of Sciences, for instance, used the Xerox machines to print clandestine *samizdat* literature.

The foundation did not have to protect itself from applicants who wanted to take advantage of it—the way I did of the Jewish Board of Guardians—because it was protected by those whom it supported. If there were any abuses, they were reported by those who regarded the foundation as their own. For instance, the foundation abandoned plans to support a charity for the production and distribution of talking books when it was alleged that the association was corrupt. This network of information made the foundation extremely efficient. With a budget of $3 million a year, it actually could offer an alternative to the Ministry of Culture, which had a much bigger budget; indeed, we became known as the alternative Ministry of Culture. One of our most successful initiatives was to support independent, student-run colleges in state-run universities and an independent students' union that later became the kernel of one of the main political parties in Hungary, Fidesz, or the Alliance of Young Democrats. The majority of their professors supported the Hungarian Democratic Forum. Being more energetic, the students prevailed over the professors. Their leader, Viktor Orbán, became prime minister in 1998.

Once in office, Orbán changed his spots. He sensed a political opportunity on the right and became increasingly nationalistic. This helped him to get reelected in 2010 and remain prime minister ever since. Orbán also became progressively more corrupt, so that Hungary can now be accurately described as a mafia state. He has also found it politically expedient to wage a media war against me, his erstwhile benefactor. He tried to turn it into a personal conflict between us, but I did not accommodate him. I always kept our differences strictly on a political level.

Coming back to the story of my Hungarian foundation, it was not without its problems. For instance, it developed a clientele that became used to receiving support, eventually making it less open to society at large than it should have been, but it escaped many of the defects that characterize normal foundations. Its success exceeded my expectations. That was the happenstance that gave me the appetite for philanthropy, which in turn provided me with a motivation to keep making money as a hedge fund manager.

In 1986, I set up a foundation in China, but I won't retell this story here because you read about it in detail in Chapter 1.

In 1987, I tried to replicate the Hungarian foundation model in Poland. I was already supporting a program for visiting Polish academics at Oxford University, and I sent money to the cultural arm of Solidarity in Poland, so we had good connections within Polish civil society. With the help of Zbigniew Pelczynski, who ran the Oxford program, we obtained the permission of the Polish authorities.

Right from the beginning, the board of the Polish foundation refused to follow the Hungarian model. It insisted that the foundation should take a more targeted approach, focusing on selected program areas instead of opening its doors wide to all kinds of proposals. I decided to give them some rope to hang themselves, but they turned out to be right, and subsequently we adopted the Polish model in other countries as well. That also taught me a lesson. I realized that the people living in the countries where I had foundations understood their country better than I did, and from then on, I deferred to the judgment of the local boards. If I seriously disagreed with their judgment, I changed the board.

I also started a foundation in the Soviet Union in 1987. In December 1986, General Secretary Mikhail Gorbachev made an unprecedented phone call to nuclear scientist and human rights activist Andrei Sakharov, who had been exiled to Gorky (now Nizhni Novgorod). Gorbachev invited him to return to Moscow "to resume your patriotic activities." I took that as a signal that something had fundamentally changed. If it had been business as usual, Sakharov might have been allowed to leave the Soviet Union but not to return to Moscow. I flew to Moscow as soon as I could.

Not long after my arrival, I identified the newly established Cultural Foundation, of which Gorbachev's wife, Raisa, was the patron, as a potential partner. I visited Sakharov and asked him to be my personal representative on the board, but he refused. "You will be merely lining the coffers of the KGB with dollars," he warned me. He took me for a naive American, and I was proud to have proved him wrong. Even so, my counterparties at the Cultural Foundation turned out to be associated with the KGB. They informed me about it in confidence when they took me for a stroll in the open air in order to avoid being overheard.

Sakharov did advise me on potential board members. I had already established contact with Tatyana Zaslavskaya, an independent-minded sociologist from Novosibirsk. Sakharov recommended Yuri Afanasiev, the historian, and Grigory Baklanov, the editor of *Znamya*, a literary magazine. I also identified the writer Daniil Granin; Valentin Rasputin, a Siberian environmentalist, who later on became ultra nationalist and one of Putin's ardent supporters; Tengiz Buachidze, a philologist from Georgia; and Boris Rauschenbakh, a space scientist and religious philosopher, as board members in whom, at that time, I could have confidence.

I made a deal with the head of the Institute of Personal Computers, who paid me for imported computers at five times the official exchange rate. And that is how my foundation in the Soviet Union, the Cultural Initiative, came into existence.

We started operating right away, without waiting for official permission. I remembered what my father had told me as a child about his experiences during the Russian Revolution: in turbulent times, the impossible becomes possible. Other Western foundations insisted on getting permission from the authorities before they started operating. For the next year or two, the Cultural Initiative was practically the only game in town, so we could make a big impact. Perhaps our most successful effort was to commission and distribute newly written textbooks in the social sciences, history, and law to high schools and universities. We also kept alive almost all the so-called thick journals—famous literary magazines like *Znamya*—that would have perished without our support.

I came up with a plan to reform the Soviet economy. Instead of geographically defined free-trade zones, I proposed freeing up a particular segment of the Soviet economy, namely the food-processing industry. I envisioned it as the embryo of a market economy embedded in the womb of the planned economy. I brought in a group of Western economists led by Wassily Leontief, a Nobel Laureate of Russian origin, and Romano Prodi, who later became president of the European Commission.

To my amazement, Premier Nikolai Ryzhkov, chairman of the Council of Ministers, ordered the heads of the various state agencies to attend our first meeting. This shows how eager the authorities were for Western assistance. I was little known at that time, yet the heads of the most powerful state agencies were lined up to meet the experts I brought. The discussions went on for a while, but it soon became clear to me that the planned economy was too diseased to support a healthy embryo.

We also brought in Western legal experts to help with the establishment of a civil code. But my ability to influence Western policy did not keep pace with the impact my foundations had in the Soviet empire. That may be attributed to a cognitive dissonance between East and West. The East was in the midst of a systemic collapse; in the West it was business as usual. When I proposed a new Marshall Plan for the Soviet empire at an East-West conference in the spring of 1989 in Potsdam, which was then still part of East Germany, I was literally laughed at. (The proposal was greeted with amusement, the *Frankfurter Allgemeine* reported.) And that was not my only attempt to influence Western policy that fell flat.

The Soviet system was rapidly disintegrating, and it was beyond the capacity of the foundation on its own to lead the transformation from a closed to an open society. Instead, the foundation itself got caught up in the process of disintegration. We discovered that some officials of the foundation were corrupt, and we lost valuable time reorganizing the leadership. We will never know what we could have accomplished had the foundation functioned properly.

I was at the very heart of the political turmoil at the time—a strange position for a foreigner. I was intimately involved in the power struggle between rival groups of economic reformers. I became very close to Grigory Yavlinsky, who tried to put into practice my father's precept—that in revolutionary times one must attempt the impossible. He was the real force behind the Shatalin Plan and the 500 Days Program, which sought to replace the Soviet Union with an economic union modeled on the European Common Market. When I brought in a group of Western economists, they were captured and practically kept prisoner for a day in a rural retreat by a rival group of reformers. I ended up taking Yavlinsky and his team to the annual meeting of the World Bank and IMF in Washington, where I helped them fight for recognition in competition with the rival team. Although I managed to get them a hearing, they went home empty handed, and Gorbachev rejected their program in favor of the less radical one. Shortly thereafter, Gorbachev himself was removed from power.

In the meantime, the Berlin Wall had fallen and the Soviet empire disintegrated. As the various Communist regimes of Eastern Europe collapsed, I followed close on their heels and established foundations in one country after another. I went to Prague with Prince Schwarzenberg, a human rights activist, just before Christmas 1989, at the height of the Velvet Revolution. We learned from the Communist Party's Marián Čalfa, who was then prime minister and acting president of Czechoslovakia, that he was determined to peacefully hand over power to Václav Havel. This came as news to Havel.

I arrived in Bucharest in early January 1990, shortly after the Communist dictator Nicolae Ceauşescu was executed. The road from the airport was lined with gun-toting soldiers, and the city itself was under siege-like conditions. I identified an opposition group and appointed the only member I could find in Bucharest as provisional president of the foundation I wanted to establish. Later on, the police infiltrated the organization, and we had to make different arrangements. From there I went on to Sofia, where an enterprising official of the US embassy had made advance arrangements for opening a Bulgarian foundation. I also traveled around in the constituent re-publics of the Soviet Union and established local founda-tions even before they became independent countries.

My visit to Ukraine was particularly memorable. I at-tended a meeting in Kiev with the cultural elite of the country, and they proposed all kinds of ideas for the foun-dation. I found all of them impractical and said so. At the end of the meeting, I apologized for responding so negatively. But they did not mind at all. "You don't real-ize how refreshing it is to have someone say no outright; our authorities always say yes and then they don't do any-thing." That was a lesson for me. From then on, I had no hesitation in rejecting proposals I found impractical.

These were hectic and euphoric times. I had a pecu-liar understanding of far-from-equilibrium conditions that I derived from my father's stories about his adventures during the Russian Revolution and my own experiences during the German occupation of Hungary. This enabled me to take advantage of the revolutionary moment.

I moved my family to London so that I could be closer to the scene of action. I distributed funds without any co-herent plan. I saw open society as a more complex form of social organization than the communist system that was collapsing. Achieving a systemic transformation required a helping hand from the outside. Everything needed to be done at once. So when I received a proposal that seemed to be backed by an ability to deliver, I usually approved it. That is how the expenditures of my Open Society Foundations ballooned from $3 million to more than $300 million in the space of a few years. It could not have been done according to a plan. We operated without a budget, and eventually the entire foundation network was running out of control. We were mired in the chaos in which we flourished. We urgently needed to introduce some order into the chaos.

A FIRMER FOOTING

I was fortunate to be able to recruit the executive director of Human Rights Watch, Aryeh Neier, to become president of the Open Society Foundations in 1993. And he took charge. I was not allowed to travel on my own anymore; somebody had to accompany me and take note of all the commitments I was making; otherwise, they would not be honored. That is when the foundation network started to take on its present shape. We established foundations under local leadership in practically every country of the former Soviet empire; these came to be known in our parlance as the "network of national foundations." We also established what we called network programs that cut across national boundaries and covered specific areas such as criminal justice, public health, education, and human rights. This created a matrix that combined local knowledge through the national foundations with professional expertise through the network programs. The matrix was open ended: national foundations could have projects outside the fields covered by network programs, and network programs could be active in countries where we had no national foundations. The Soviet system continued to disintegrate, but our organization started to become more cohesive. The chaotic years had served their purpose. The foundations had been first on the scene and earned a reputation for their willingness to attempt the impossible. Now their work became more professional.

About a third of our budget was spent on education—bringing a child-centered approach emphasizing critical thinking to a region used to authoritarian methods and rote learning. I established the Central European University, a postgraduate institution, first in Prague and then in Budapest, with a branch in Warsaw. Its history is detailed in Chapter 3 of this book. I also set up a Higher Education Support Program, which spent about an equal amount of money on other newly established educational institutions, reforming the curricula of state universities, and providing fellowships to faculty at public universities to enable scholars to go for study trips to the west and additional salary to motivate them to return to their home universities. In addition, we supported systemic reform both in higher and general education. And we introduced Step by Step for preschool-age children, which was a modification of the Head Start program for kindergarten.

Another third or more of our budget went to support civil society in the broadest sense, with particular emphasis on civil rights and the protection of vulnerable populations. We identified the gypsies—or Roma, as they are now called—as the worst case of social exclusion on ethnic grounds in Eastern Europe, and we devoted increasing amounts of money and energy to deal with the problem—at first supporting their culture and then their education. Our greatest achievement was to raise a new generation of educated young Roma who were proud to be Roma.

As the disintegration of the Soviet system continued and the suffering of the population increased, so did our budget. I devoted $100 million to establish an International Science Foundation whose objective was to preserve the best of Soviet science from destruction. It distributed emergency grants of $500 each to the most eminent scientists in the former Soviet Union. Due to runaway inflation, that was enough to support a family for a year. Selection was based on a simple and objective criterion: three citations in an internationally recognized scientific journal. More than thirty thousand scientists qualified. The rest of the money was spent on research programs selected by an international jury of scientists, using the peer-review system. The scheme was an outstanding success: the entire amount was committed within a year.

My objective was not only to save the best of Soviet natural science, which I considered one of the crowning achievements of the human intellect, but also to demonstrate that foreign aid could be administered efficiently. In a *Wall Street Journal* article in 1992, I proposed that the aid offered by the IMF should be administered along the same lines. Instead of providing budgetary support to the

Soviet government and its successors, the aid should be earmarked for the payment of pensions and unemployment benefits and its distribution closely supervised. The idea was a good one, but it did not go anywhere. Generally speaking, when I implemented an idea on my own, it worked; when I tried to influence public policy, I did not get very far. This has changed with the passage of time: more recently, I have been more successful in mobilizing public support.

I firmly believe that if my *Wall Street Journal* proposal had been followed, history would have taken a different course. The people of the Soviet Union would have seen some practical and tangible benefits from Western aid, and their attitude toward the West would be quite different. Europe is paying a heavy price today for having failed to come to the assistance of the Russian people in their hour of need.

I also matured a lot in the course of these adventures. At first, I was carried away by the almost unlimited opportunities opened up by the collapse of the Soviet system, and I was so eager to play a role in history that I did not hesitate to attempt the impossible. Gradually, I learned to discern between what could work and what could not. I became more discriminating and concerned with achieving something worthwhile. I remember a visit to Moscow when two of the most important people I was supposed to meet canceled their appointment with me because of some statement I made. Earlier, I would have been upset;

now I felt good about the stand I took. More recently, when people asked me whether I have met Putin, I could honestly say I did not want to.

The year 1992 brought an important change in my status as a public figure. When sterling was forced out of the European Exchange Rate Mechanism, I became known as "the man who broke the Bank of England." This happened because I did not deny that my hedge fund had played a role in the event; the media then exaggerated my role. I deliberately allowed it to happen in order to establish a platform from which I could speak out on other issues. And it worked. Suddenly I had a voice that could be heard.

That year Yugoslavia was caught up in civil war, and I used my platform to announce a $50 million fund for humanitarian assistance to the civilian population of war-torn Bosnia. My announcement at Christmastime drew attention to their plight. The original idea behind my donation was to get aid workers into the war zone, which in turn would compel the United Nations troops to adopt more aggressive rules of engagement to protect them. That is not what happened. UN troops did not intervene to prevent the massacre at Srebrenica. But a genius of humanitarian assistance, a Texan named Fred Cuny, used the money to provide gas, electricity, and water for Sarajevo as well as seeds for growing vegetables. The idea behind my contribution didn't work, but the way Fred Cuny used my money did. It may not be an exaggeration to say that it helped the people of Sarajevo to survive. Shortly thereafter,

Cuny was killed in Chechnya in circumstances that were never clarified, and his body was never recovered.

I visited Sarajevo in November 1993 when the city was under siege. I did it reluctantly because I was not eager to put my life at risk. It was a pretty scary trip, flying in an Ilyushin Il-76, one of the world's largest planes. We were sitting next to stacks of gas pipes lying on the floor. The Ukrainian crew was tightening and loosening the straps that held the pipes together as the plane was banking and landing. Then we had ten minutes to clear the airport.

I went to Sarajevo for a ceremonial opening of the water plant that Fred Cuny had built. It had been flown in by plane in modules and installed into a road tunnel in the side of a mountain. But the local authorities did not give permission for the water to be turned on. We never found out why. Either somebody was making a lot of money selling water or the government wanted to continue having people killed by snipers while waiting for water in order to have pictures on TV generating sympathy for the city's plight. Or both. I had to threaten to go public with my protest before permission to turn on the spigots was granted.

The task of putting a semblance of order to the foundations that had sprung up across Eastern Europe and the former Soviet Union was an arduous one but not as all-absorbing or enjoyable as the revolutionary period. Our annual spending peaked around $600 million before we started introducing fiscal discipline. The goal was to cut spending in half, but it was never reached because new

opportunities arose elsewhere. But before starting that
story, let me first finish my story about the Soviet Union.

CHALLENGES

When Putin came to power in 1999, our foundation in
Russia came under attack and was effectively chased out
of the country. We had rented a building with an option
to buy. However, the Russian mafia managed to replace
the contract deposited at the court with a forged one from
which the option to buy was removed. We had to leave
our office when the lease expired. At the time, I was not
sure whether this was the work of the Russian mafia, but
in retrospect I am more inclined to believe that it had the
connivance of the authorities.

One of the reasons why President Putin came to regard me as a personal enemy was my support for Mikheil
Saakashvili in Georgia in the early 2000s. That is a sad
story as far as I am concerned. During the presidency of
Eduard Shevardnadze, Georgia became very corrupt. A
major anticorruption campaign was launched by a group
of reformers led by Saakashvili, who was the minister of
justice at the time, and Zurab Zhvania, who was president
of the parliament. It was supported by my foundation, and
I became personally involved. It was also supported by
President Shevardnadze, whom I considered a decent person but burnt out. The anticorruption program itself was
well formulated and ambitious, but it could not get off the

ground. Every time I visited Georgia, President Shevard-nadze made a gesture of support, but he could never deliver because the main source of corruption was the Ministry of Interior, and his life literally depended on the security services. Eventually the reformers lost their patience. Saakashvili and Zhvania left the government and formed a political party in opposition to President Shevardnadze. I expressed my support for them by giving them the 2003 Open Society Prize on behalf of the Central European University. The opposition was successful at the polls in November. An independent exit poll, supported by my foundation among others, gave them a clear majority, but the official results declared the government party as the winner. The people believed the exit polls, not the official results, and there was a revolution. Saakashvili became president in January 2004.

I was elated and did whatever I could to help him succeed. I donated several million dollars to a capacity-building fund set up by the United Nations Development Program that paid supplemental salaries of a thousand dollars a month to members of Saakashvili's cabinet and a hundred dollars a month to the police force. This allowed Saakashvili to impose discipline on the police and order them to remove the road blocks where they extorted bribes from the passing traffic. This was a tangible anticorruption measure that greatly enhanced his popularity. But the situation deteriorated when the Saakashvili administration arrested a large number of prominent businessmen on corruption charges and extorted large sums of money from them for their release. The monies went into a slush fund that was used for the purchase of arms to defend Georgia against an expected attack by Russia. Being a slush fund, it eventually became a source of corruption.

My foundation in Georgia spoke out against this lawless behavior, and in the absence of a parliamentary opposition, it became the most vocal critic of the new government. I personally was at first inclined to be more tolerant of the government's excesses, arguing that in revolutionary situations, the normal rules don't apply, but when they did not cease, I also became more critical. Saakashvili in power turned out to be much less of a paragon of opensociety values than he had been in opposition.

In the meantime, I was accused by the Russian media of being Saakashvili's pay master, and Putin advised the rulers of the Central Asian republics to close down my foundations. Fortunately, most of them decided against it, but the foundations felt the pressure, and there were adverse repercussions in other parts of the world as well. This was a painful lesson that taught me to keep a greater distance personally from the internal politics of the countries where I have foundations.

That conclusion is easier to reach in theory than to implement in practice. The strategy we have developed to deal with individual countries greatly depends on internal political conditions. We take a two-pronged approach. On the one hand, we help civil society to hold governments accountable. On the other, we try to work with those governments that are willing to accept our help. We can be more effective if we can exercise both functions, and we can be most effective at times of democratic regime change when a new government is eager to establish a more open society but does not have the capacity to do so. Strengthening their capacity is often our greatest contribution. That is what we did when the Soviet system collapsed. We brought in foreign expertise and provided financial support to qualified nationals of the countries concerned to return from abroad. And that is what we did a decade later in Georgia. When I look back on that difficult experience, I am not sure whether I would want to do anything differently.

The real lesson I learned in Georgia is that helping countries in transition is a difficult and thankless task. We have had similar experiences elsewhere, where systemic reforms introduced by one government were systematically undone by the next one. Russia is the prime example. The freedoms that prevailed during the chaotic Yeltsin years have all but disappeared under Putin. Still, there is a more subtle lesson to be learned. It is dangerous to build systemic reforms on a close association with one particular government. Systemic reforms need broad public participation and support. That is what makes them irreversible.

There was another reason why Putin considered me his personal enemy: I published a long article in the *New York Review of Books* in 2000 in which I revealed the way Boris Berezovsky helped elect Putin as president. He allegedly hired some Chechen terrorists to blow up entire apartment houses in Moscow, killing some three hundred inhabitants in their sleep. In the panic that followed, fear and anger were directed against the Chechens, assisted by a carefully orchestrated campaign in the press and on television. The invasion of Chechnya and the Duma elections were held in an atmosphere of war hysteria. Very few presidential candidates dared to oppose the invasion. Those who did were wiped out. Yevgeni Primakov, who had been considered the favorite candidate for the presidency, was decisively defeated. Using the momentum generated by the victory in the parliamentary elections, Yeltsin, who was under Berezovsky's control, announced his resignation on New Year's Eve, and Primakov withdrew from the contest, assuring the election of Putin as his successor. Reading my article made Putin very angry. But he did not feel secure enough to attack the foundation directly because it was very popular. He found the round-about way I described earlier. Later on, Putin chased Berezovsky out of the country; he took refuge in London.

Berezovsky claimed that he had incriminating evidence against Putin: one of his underlings allegedly had participated in blowing up the apartment houses in Moscow. Berezovsky spirited the eye witness out of Russia and presented him at a press conference in London. But the event was ignored by the media and by heads of state, who did not want to acknowledge Putin's guilt. (Who would want to shake hands with a president who had the blood of his compatriots on his hands?)

I decided to wind up the Russian foundation in 2003. Clearly, the Russian government did not deserve our continued assistance and did not tolerate our presence. We found other ways to support our grantees. In 2015, we were declared to be an "undesirable" organization and any Russian citizen dealing with us faced penalties ranging from fines to a maximum of six years in prison.

It was a rather sad ending to a valiant philanthropic effort, but I have no regrets. It is obvious that we failed to help Russia make the transition from a closed to an open society. But at least we tried. I continue to believe that if the Western governments had followed my advice, history would have taken a different course. I also believe that in philanthropy, one should do the right thing, whether or not it succeeds. That is the big difference between philanthropic and business investments. I am certain that the work of the foundation was appreciated by the Russian people at the time, and it will have a positive influence in the long run in spite of all the adverse propaganda directed against us by the Putin regime.

NEW OPPORTUNITIES

Let me now turn to the new opportunities that prevented us from reducing our global spending. In 1994, the apartheid system was abandoned in South Africa and Nelson Mandela became president. Given our history in South Africa, I felt obliged to set up a national foundation in South Africa. From there we branched out to other parts of Africa, and our network programs also started to reach

out to other parts of the world. Also in 1994, the Duva-
lier regime was overturned in Haiti and American troops
occupied the country; I felt this called for establishing a
foundation there. Aryeh Neier knew just the right person,
Michèle Pierre-Louis, to run it. Later, Aryeh also knew
a good person for Guatemala, where the long civil war
ended in 1996, offering an opportunity for a transition
to democracy. We set up a foundation there whose board
had a unique character: it combined urban liberal intel-
lectuals with leaders of indigenous communities from the
countryside.

By 1995, I felt that we had done enough on the first
point of our agenda—opening up closed societies—so that
we could pass on to the second: making open societies
more viable. The activities of the Open Society Foundations were concentrated in foreign countries; it was time
to do something at home. I reflected on the deficiencies
of open society in America and developed a strategic plan
that I then submitted to a select group of social philosophers for critical examination. They included Seyla Ben-
habib, Leon Botstein, Aryeh Neier, David Rothman, Alan
Ryan, Tim Scanlon, and Bernard Williams.

Two ideas were novel. First, market values had pene-
trated into areas where they did not properly belong; most
notably they had undermined professional values. Liberal
professions like medicine, law, and journalism had been
turned into businesses. The primacy of professional values needed to be reaffirmed. Second, in certain areas fear
stifled the critical process and gave rise to false dogmas

characterized by prejudice and intolerance, which undermine the principles of open society. I identified two such areas: the American attitudes toward death and to drug policy. They have something in common: both drug addiction and death constitute insoluble problems, and there is an understandable inclination to look for false solutions. Many of the solutions make the problems worse than they need be. In both cases they involve a refusal to accept the existence of an insoluble problem: doctors prolong life at all cost, and drug warriors advocate zero tolerance.

The rest of our programs in the United States were the outgrowth of our programs in the rest of the world: social justice, vulnerable populations, civil rights, and the criminal justice system. The strategy passed critical examination, and we started implementing it. I concerned myself mainly with the two new ideas I had introduced. I was happy to delegate the other areas to Aryeh Neier, who knew a lot more about them than I did.

The Project on Death in America was perhaps our most successful domestic program. It gave life to a new field: end-of-life care. The American attitude of denial applied both to the medical profession and to the general public. We found a group of experts who knew how to deal with dying patients, and they transformed the care of terminal patients into a medical discipline by establishing fellowships at various medical institutions. They helped enlighten the general public more indirectly. The most effective effort was a five-part television series on public television by Bill Moyers. That was not financed by the

Open Society Foundations, but Moyers drew heavily on work sponsored by us. Dying ceased to be a taboo subject. We celebrated our success by withdrawing from the field when other foundations moved in. But more recently we reentered the field by cosponsoring a second generation of projects that were spawned by the first one.

With drug policy, we faced a much greater challenge because the United States remained in the grip of drug-war hysteria until President Obama became more of an ally than an opponent of drug-policy reform in his last years in the White House.

I was convinced that the war on drugs did more harm than drugs themselves, but I was reluctant to advocate legalization as a solution. It would have helped the drug warriors who wanted to present drug policy as an either/or issue. We therefore embraced "harm reduction" as our guiding principle, aiming to reduce the harm done both by drug use and by failed prohibitionist policies. Even so, the drug legalizers tried to paint me as a legalizer.

Just as the war on drugs had driven mass incarceration in the 1980s and 1990s, so drug-policy reform became the cutting edge of efforts to reduce incarceration. We concentrated on marijuana, which accounted for half of all the arrests. I supported, with other philanthropists, a successful medical marijuana initiative in California in 1996. We followed it up with another ballot initiative, in 2000, to require treatment instead of incarceration for low-level drug offenders. That temporarily stalled the rapid growth in the state's prison population and created a model that other states began to emulate. Other victories followed, notably reform of New York's draconian Rockefeller drug laws and other mandatory-minimum drug-sentencing laws. By 2008, America's incarceration rate began to fall at last. Public support for legalizing marijuana for all adults steadily increased. When Colorado and Washington voted in 2012 to legally regulate marijuana, they became the first jurisdictions in the world to do so, which was all the more remarkable because the United States had for so long been the chief promoter and enforcer of the global war on drugs. Now marijuana is legal for medical purposes in over thirty states and for all adults in ten, with others sure to follow. Our focus has now shifted to ensuring that those people and communities who were most harmed by the drug war receive a fair share of the benefits of legalization.

Progress on the public health aspects of harm reduction has been steady but all too slow. Ensuring legal access to sterile syringes is crucial to reducing HIV and other infectious diseases, which is why we became the principal private supporter of programs and advocacy efforts in this area in the late 1990s, both in the United States and abroad. This was supplemented some years later by efforts to stem the rapidly growing epidemic of overdose fatalities involving pharmaceutical opioids, heroin, and, now, fentanyl. We focused on increasing access to naloxone (the antidote to an opioid overdose), passing 911 "Good Samaritan" laws to protect drug users who call 911, and, more recently, supporting advocacy for opening "safe consumption rooms," which reduce risk of fatal overdose, infections, and other health problems.

The drug problem has changed dramatically since the early 2000s, when opioid misuse and overdose fatalities began to rise precipitously. Producers and distributors of legal opioids—notably including the Sackler family's Purdue Pharma—have been severely criticized, but unscrupulous doctors have also promoted their distribution. Attempts to discourage over-prescribing—including forced tapering of patients dependent on opioids, changing medicine formulations to prevent injection, and tracking and limiting prescriptions—are backfiring, driving too many users to illegal street drugs containing fentanyl, which is far more powerful than heroin and responsible for most overdose increases.

In contrast with previous spikes in overdose deaths, whose victims were mainly African and Hispanic Americans, the current crisis has also hit rural white populations. Since they constitute Trump's heartland, he has an incentive to bring the epidemic under control, but he is following misguided policies. He has failed to crack down on the perpetrators and to take effective measures to help the victims; imposing coercive treatment and prosecutions for fentanyl distribution don't work.

On the health side, increasing harm-reduction measures—including many used in Europe but not permitted in the United States—ought to be the focus. We must think creatively about the interplay of multiple factors, such as pharmaceutical business interests, extremes of over-prescription and over-control, economic hardships caused by overpriced drugs, and a black market for drugs.

On the criminal justice front, my priority going forward is to build support in the United States for decriminalizing drug possession as Portugal and some other European countries have done. And eventually, having learned from cannabis regulation, we will tackle the challenge of regulating other drugs in ways that minimize the harms of prohibitionist policies without inviting significant increases in drug-use problems.

The project to reaffirm professional values had mixed results. In the legal profession, we have been very successful in establishing individual fellowships for practicing public-service law but much less successful in promoting professional standards in the selection of judges. The process has become even more politicized. In journalism, we sponsored several initiatives in investigative journalism, but otherwise we made little progress in addressing the problems of a profession that is essential to an open society and is in the midst of a technological transformation. In medicine, we established an institute for protecting the medical profession from the enticements of the pharmaceutical industry, but we have not been able to modify the mercenary attitude prevailing in professional associations and among some doctors. The recent debate on healthcare legislation has demonstrated how little public understanding there is about the meaning of healthcare. The American system provides payment for medical procedures, not for preventive healthcare. The national healthcare systems of Europe and Canada do a better job in spite of their imperfections, but universal healthcare remained a nonstarter in America until the midterm elections in 2018. Universal healthcare became an important plank in the Democratic platform for 2020, although there is a sharp division between progressive and moderate Democrats, and it continues to be denounced by Republicans as socialism.

My interest in the shortcomings of America as an open society and my concern about the failure of the West to provide assistance to the former Soviet Union led me to study the deficiencies of global capitalism. In February 1997, I wrote an article for the *Atlantic Monthly* entitled "The Capitalist Threat" that questioned the precepts of the Washington consensus. After the emerging market crisis of 1997, I expanded it into a book under the title *The Crisis of Global Capitalism*. In 2000, I wrote another book, *On Globalization*, where I advocated a set of reforms, but they were not taken seriously. One of these reforms, namely the use of Special Drawing Rights, was actually adopted, but only after the crash of 2008.

A GLOBAL NETWORK

In the twenty-first century, the Open Society Foundations went global. It would have been unwieldy to establish national foundations all over the world, so we started establishing regional foundations—one for Southern Africa, covering the nine countries belonging to the Southern African Development Community (SADC); one for the eighteen countries in Western Africa belonging to the Economic Union of Western African States (ECOWAS); and one for Eastern Africa, covering first Kenya and slowly expanding to the neighboring countries.

When Suharto fell, we established a foundation in Indonesia in 2000. After the invasion of Afghanistan, we established a foundation there as well as one in Pakistan. The Afghan foundation grew strong, but in Pakistan our fate depends on which government is in power. Our legal registration has been withdrawn and our continued functioning hangs on a thread. We had a small number of grants in Iraq as well. In other parts of the world—notably the Middle East, Southeast Asia, and Latin America—our initial efforts were less formal, but as our engagement grew, it resulted in the establishment of regional foundations.

In addition to the open matrix that combines national foundations with network programs, we also opened up a new dimension that I call "the network of networks." This involves establishing independent organizations with their own governing board, leadership, and staff with whom we maintain close cooperation. This has become my favorite formula for entering new fields of activity because their ability to raise funds from others establishes a quasi-objective standard of performance that we lack in our wholly owned foundations network. Our financial support ought, in theory, not to exceed one-third of the total budget so that they maintain their independence. In practice, it usually takes several years to reach that target. This approach has been very successful. It has spawned organizations such as Global Witness, the International Crisis Group (ICG), and, more recently, the European Council of Foreign Relations (ECFR), and the Institute for New Economic Thinking (INET). There are many other less well-known or more recent ones.

In 2011, when I first published a version of this essay, I surveyed the foundation network. I was, on the whole, satisfied, but I had two big concerns. The first was what would happen to the foundation when the president, Aryeh Neier, and I were no longer around? Second, and more importantly, what more could we still accomplish during my lifetime?

When I established the foundation, I did not want it to survive me. The fate of other institutions has taught me that they tend to stray very far from the founder's intentions. But as the foundation took on a more substantial form, I changed my mind. I came to realize that terminating it at the time of my death would be an act of excessive selfishness, the equivalent to burning an Indian Maharajah's wives on his funeral pyre. A number of very capable people are devoting their lives to the work of the foundation, and I have no right to pull the rug from under them.

More importantly, we have identified and specialized in a sphere of activity that needs to be carried on beyond my lifetime and whose execution does not really require my presence. That niche consists in empowering civil society to hold governments accountable. In the United States, there are some institutions, like the American Civil Liberties Union, devoted to the task, but in most other countries, there aren't any. In many countries, wealthy people are too dependent on the government to be able to provide such support, nor are they motivated to do so. Hence the niche for us. I have also identified some other activities, such as protecting vulnerable populations and providing legal protection for the poor, that fall in the same category. These are worthy objectives, and the foundations ought to be able to serve them beyond my lifetime.

What will be missing when I am gone is the entrepreneurial and innovative spirit that has characterized us. I have tried to deal with problems as they arose. I was able to move fast and take big risks. The governing board that will succeed me will not be able to follow my example; it will be weighed down by fiduciary responsibilities. Some of its members will try to be faithful to the founder's intentions; others will be risk averse, but the founder, who spends the money he made, is anything but risk averse.

The original structure of the Open Society Foundations was far too complicated to be preserved in its existing form. As I noted before, our growth had been entirely unplanned. During the period of explosive growth, when our

spending went from $3 million to $300 million, we didn't
even have a budget. Then Aryeh Neier came on board and
brought some order into the chaos. He established a very
elaborate budget process that takes a long time to prepare
and has to start much in advance. I never took much interest in it; I was much more interested in rising to the
occasion when an opportunity presented itself. As a result,
Aryeh and I had two very different types of foundations
combined in one: the initiatives in which I was directly
involved continued to run on a very elastic budget, and the
organization headed by Aryeh ran on a very tight budget.
As the initiatives matured, they passed from my hands into
his. By contrast, the human and civil rights and criminal
justice areas had been fully in his hands since inception.

Ours had been a very productive partnership, but it had
resulted in a very unruly structure that would have been
unmanageable in our absence. We felt we must reorganize
it while we were around. A new president would have had
to spend several years just to get to know the organization.
As it turned out, the task of reorganization has fallen to
the new management that took charge in 2018, and they
are making good progress in getting it done.

I couldn't give a proper accounting of the far-reaching
and varied activities going on inside because I am not
aware of all of them. When I was younger, I used to travel
around the foundation network all the time, and I was
greatly inspired by what I saw. The activities of which I
was not aware were often the best; it was the problematic
ones that were brought to my attention.

The foundations have grown organically by responding to needs and opportunities as they arose. In my opinion, that is the right way. Many other foundations are engaged in meeting their own institutional needs. We try to resist that. We pride ourselves on being a "selfless foundation," and that has been a source of strength for us. We have been able to cooperate with other foundations, and we have accomplished a lot more by *not* claiming ownership of the projects. Other institutions need to produce successes in order to raise funds; we are satisfied by actually accomplishing something, whether or not it is recognized. Paradoxically, this has gained us more friends and allies than beating our own drum. But there is a downside as well: since we don't advertise our successes, others don't do it for us either.

We have been successful in moving where the action is. In each country, we start with supporting critical thinking or dissident activity, and we move in quickly when a new government comes to power that has good intentions but lacks the capacity to deliver. And we have been more persistent than official aid agencies in maintaining a presence long after they have moved on to greener pastures. The same is true of issues of global governance: we are not always the first to recognize them, but once we become aware of them, we remain committed to them, be it climate change, drug policy, or the Global Fund to Fight AIDS, Tuberculosis, and Malaria.

Our main difficulty has been in keeping our network of national foundations and "legacy" programs from going stale. That requires almost as much effort as starting new ones, yet my preference has been to focus on the cutting edge. Going forward, I favor the "network of networks" format.

THE FUTURE

Having decided to allow the Open Society Foundations to survive me, I have done my best to prepare them for my absence. But I realize that I am bound to fail because if I fully succeeded, it would contradict my principle of fallibility. Therefore, I bequeath my successors the task of revising any of the arrangements I shall have left behind as long as they do it in the same spirit in which I have made them.

I see great opportunities open to the foundations. It is true that we have many enemies and detractors in many parts of the world, and there is a whole industry engaged in demonizing me. But we have established a solid track record of being genuinely concerned with the well-being of humanity, and we have an active involvement with many of the burning issues of the day. I am ready to contribute when we have something valuable to offer, even if that requires invading the principal of our endowment.

On a personal level, I'm very proud of my enemies. When I look at the list, I feel I must be doing something right. Still, I wish the list would be shorter; I and my foundations will do our best to shorten it.

In conclusion, let me return to the question I raised at the beginning: A selfish man with a selfless foundation—how do the two fit together?

Here is the explanation.

I formed a rather negative view of foundations when I was a supplicant, and I have not changed my mind since I became a philanthropist. There is something inherently self-contradictory in altruism, but most foundations see no need to recognize it and even less to resolve it. When you are giving away money, the recipients flatter you and do everything they can to make you feel good, so the contradictions are obscured by a thick layer of hypocrisy. That is what makes me leery of philanthropy. The foundations set the rules, and others have to live by them. Applicants can, of course, have their own way. They can tell the foundation what it wants to hear and then proceed to do what they want to do. Remember my encounter with the Jewish Board of Guardians?

Well, I have resolved the seeming contradiction between a self-centered philanthropist and a selfless foundation. It is my consciousness that has made me self-aware, and it has also made me aware of how inadequate my mortal self is as the sole beneficiary of my consciousness. In other words, I have a very big ego—far too big for my mortal self. I can find sufficient scope for it only by identifying with something more enduring. Helping a few people around me as my father did is not enough for me;

what he did retail I want to do wholesale. I aspire to make the world a better place by enabling people to change it. That is where my conceptual framework comes into play. It is both the product of my inflated ego and the source of the systemic reforms I advocate. If I have gained some special insights, then I am under a special obligation to put them to good use. The fact that I am rich adds to my sense of duty. There are people who are rich, people with insights, and people who care about humanity, but rarely are the three qualifications combined in one person. Only that combination satisfies my ambition.

I also need to explain the relationship between my philosophy and my ego. At first, they were entangled in a knot. When I first started writing about reflexivity, I was inseparably attached to the idea because it was mine. I could not part with it. I kept on getting more and more convoluted in trying to articulate it until one morning I couldn't understand what I had written the night before. It took me most of my life to separate my ego from my philosophy, and both have benefited from it. Today, my philosophy finds expression both in my writings and in my foundations, and my ego can sit back and enjoy them.

Since my philanthropy is a source of ego satisfaction, I feel I do not deserve any thanks for it. Indeed, I used to be embarrassed by expressions of gratitude. I felt that the enlarged ego responsible for my philanthropy would not have been socially acceptable if I had flaunted it; therefore, it was embarrassing to be thanked for it. But I don't feel that way anymore. I realize that I have in fact helped a large number of people. That is what people see, not my enlarged ego. Therefore, it is natural that they want to thank me. I have learnt to accept their gratitude. At the same time, I no longer see any reason to feel ashamed of having such a large ego because it turned out to be beneficial not only to me, but also to many others. But a large ego is difficult to satisfy. Having seen through the hypocrisy that surrounds philanthropy, I cannot be satisfied by praise and flattery. They leave me cold. I need to see actual accomplishments. That is how a selfish man came to have a selfless foundation.

I still find the large gap between who I am and how I am seen by others both fascinating and disturbing. That is why I feel driven to go through with these explanations. I regard altruism and philanthropy not as a duty but as a pleasure and a source of satisfaction. It is a luxury that rich people can afford. I much prefer philanthropy to, say, collecting art. It has connected me with other people and allowed me to break out of my isolation. An art collection could not do that for me. The day I had a panic attack on Leadenhall Street I did not think it was worth dying for the sake of amassing wealth. Since then, I have been occasionally exposed to mortal danger in connection with my foundation activities. I do not seek such danger, but I am willing to accept it. And it gives me a sense of satisfaction to be engaged in an activity for which it would be worth dying.

I occupy an exceptional position. My success in the financial markets has given me a greater degree of independence than most other people. This allows me to take a stand on controversial issues. In fact, it obliges me to do so because other rich people are often hindered by their business interests from taking controversial positions. The success of my hedge fund has made me independent of my investors. This gives me the added satisfaction of feeling that I enjoy an exceptional position.

In short, my philanthropy has made me happy. What more could one ask for? I do not feel, however, that I have any business imposing my choice on others. That is why I did not join Bill Gates and Warren Buffett in their campaign urging rich people to give away half their wealth, especially as I believe that the value of philanthropy lies not in the amount of money devoted to it but on how it is spent.

Clearly, I am not a saint, nor do I aspire to be one. I cannot think of anything more unnatural and unrewarding than to be selfless. By contrast, I consider a selfless foundation extremely valuable. Most people participate in public affairs with selfish motives. They tend to cling to whatever power and influence they have attained, and it is often difficult to remove them when they stand in the way of a satisfactory solution.

There are two obstacles to finding the optimum arrangements: one is imperfect understanding; the other is the influence of special interests that are in conflict with the common interest. A selfless foundation is subject to the first limitation but is exempt from the second. And that gives it great scarcity value.

I have made it a principle to pursue my self-interest in my business, subject only to legal and ethical limitations, and to serve the public interest as a public intellectual and philanthropist. If the two are in conflict, I make sure that the public interest prevails. I do not hesitate to advocate policies that are in conflict with my business interests. And I firmly believe that our democracy would function better if a few more people adopted this principle. And if they care about a well-functioning democracy, they ought to abide by this principle, even if others do not do so. Even a few people could make a big difference. They would help make the world a better place.

CHAPTER 3

The Central European University (CEU) and Its Future

"A University That Takes Its Principles and Its Social Responsibilities Seriously"

I established the Central European University (CEU) as a graduate school for the social sciences and humanities in 1991.

Under the Soviet system, scientists were kept segregated in academies of science. Considered to be critics of the regime, most of them were not allowed to teach at universities because the regime was afraid they would poison the minds of students with their quest for freedom of thought and research. Promising science students in elite schools had the chance to get admitted to scientific academies, but once there, they were typically kept away from teaching. As the regime weakened, the clamor of social scientists to gain access to students increased.

The first breach in this segregation occurred in Tito's Yugoslavia in 1970. The rector of Zagreb University, Ivan Supek, a physicist and a former student of Werner Heisenberg, established the Inter-University Center (IUC) in Dubrovnik. IUC invited academics and students from East and West. Since Yugoslavia was a nonaligned nation, those from the East had a better chance of getting permission to travel to Dubrovnik than, say, to Oxford. Supek also visited Bill Newton-Smith, a philosopher of science, who was then in charge of graduate students at Balliol College in Oxford and later became the first de facto president of CEU. Supek asked Newton-Smith to attract Western participants to IUC, especially from Oxford.

IUC flourished. I heard about it from Newton-Smith, and it piqued my interest. I provided him with funds to increase the participation from Oxford, and from the middle of the 1980s, I also provided scholarships to students and fellowships to scholars from Eastern Europe to take part in the summer programs. I visited Dubrovnik in April 1989, just months before the fall of the Berlin Wall. I attended classes, talked to students and faculty both from East and West, and liked what I saw. In the evenings, I met with the attending professors, who were mainly from Communist countries. They all urged me to set up a new graduate university that would bridge the gap between them and the students they wanted to teach. The only point of disagreement was the location of the university. Not surprisingly, Hungarians argued for Budapest, Czechs for Prague, and Poles for Warsaw. It became clear that a Central European University would need to have three campuses.

The idea appealed to me, but I hesitated. Until then, I had specialized in reorienting the activities of existing institutions, such as the Karl Marx University of Economics in Budapest, or reforming social science curricula taught at Eastern European universities, not establishing new institutions. I didn't like to spend money on bricks and mortar.

Establishing a new university with three campuses was an expensive proposition. I did not want to be the sole sponsor, not merely on account of the expense but, more importantly, on principle: having a sole sponsor would endanger the independence of the institution. From then on, I followed the same principle in establishing other institutions like Crisis Group, the European Council on Foreign Relations (ECFR), and the Institute for New Economic

Thinking (INET): I tried to limit my contribution to one-third.

But trying to avoid spending money on buildings turned out to be a big mistake, as I soon discovered. The Czech prime minister, Petr Pithart, offered us a ten-story building under construction but near completion in Prague. It had been intended for use by the trade unions, but they were politically discredited in the post-revolutionary transition period. We discovered that part of the building had been offered to the Center for Economic Research and Graduate Education led by Jan Svejnar, a Czech economist who had recently returned from America. We soon found an amicable agreement. The Center became the economics department of CEU, and for a time it was the best-run one. Unfortunately, Pithart was defeated the following year, and his place was taken by Václav Klaus, a neoliberal, market fundamentalist economist who considered me a socialist. We became lifelong enemies.

In January 1993, at the moment of the dissolution of Czechoslovakia, Klaus said that an optical illusion has finally disappeared from the map: the Czech Republic has nothing to do with Central Europe anymore. One of his first acts was to kick us out of the building.

The Slovak government had also promised me a building at the same time as Petr Pithart, but when I wanted to take up the offer, it turned out that the building was meant to serve as the Slovak Parliament. The government offered us another site where a new university could be built from scratch, but that would have taken too long for me. I wanted the university to take advantage of the revolutionary moment and start operating right away.

Erhard Busek, vice chancellor of Austria, was a great believer in the open society. He wanted to attract CEU to Vienna, but when we took a closer look at the offer, we found that it consisted of scholarships and various in-kind services. We would have to buy our own building. (It is ironic that twenty-five years later, we find ourselves in the same situation in Vienna.)

Fortunately, the Polish government had no buildings to offer. Our partner, the School of Sociology, which enjoyed an international reputation, became the sociology department of CEU. That left us with Hungary.

The Hungarian government offered us the Young Pioneer Camp because there were no young pioneers anymore. It was a beautiful pastoral site located in a woody area in the hills above Buda. Bill Newton-Smith was very excited about it, but it was about an hour's commute from the center of town, and the Hungarian supporters of CEU argued that in the outskirts of the city the new university would be both spatially and intellectually marginalized.

According to an agreement the Hungarian Soros Foundation had signed with the Hungarian authorities in 1984, the government promised to support joint reform projects by providing annually the forint equivalent of every dollar I spent over $3 million in Hungary. But the huge budgetary deficit of the government and the indebtedness of the country prevented the government from fulfilling its promise. When we started looking for a suitable building in Budapest, the government proposed that, in lieu of its financial obligations, it would contribute to the purchase of a state-owned building for the university. This is how we ended up owning a small aristocratic palace in downtown Budapest that the government agreed to sell us. The palace had served as the headquarters of military intelligence after World War II, so we were not surprised when we found spyholes on the doors in the cellars. This is where the most important war criminals were kept in prison during their trial, among them Ferenc Szálasi, the head of the Arrow Cross, the Hungarian Nazi Party, who was later publicly executed.

By 1994, I realized what a serious mistake I had made in expecting governments to provide CEU with buildings. I bought about half of the buildings in that centrally located block and got permission to build a modern high-rise in the middle of the block.

I also realized how important it is for a university to have a home that it can be proud of. Several years later, during the tenure of John Shattuck, an international legal scholar, human rights protector, and diplomat, as rector, we engaged an outstanding Irish architectural studio, O'Donnel+Tumey. They won the Royal Institute of British Architects' Gold Medal, while Sheila O'Donnel was chosen Woman Architect of the Year 2019 for her work on the CEU campus.

―――――

The idea of a new university in the social sciences and humanities was enthusiastically supported by the new liberal politicians, who had fought the Communist regime in the previous decades. The list included Václav Havel; Árpád Göncz, the newly elected president of Hungary; and Bronislaw Geremek, a renowned medieval studies scholar and the future Polish foreign minister.

Neither I nor the people I entrusted with establishing the university knew how to do it. It was amateur hour. The first problem was to gain accreditation. It would have been a long, drawn out process, and I wanted CEU to start operating immediately. A member of the executive committee, Paul Flather, came up with an ingenious idea. He discovered that there were no universities in Luxemburg at the time, and consequently, the use of the word "university" was not legally restricted. We were able to create a foundation in Luxembourg called Central European University and printed impressive-looking documents attesting to this fact. This allowed us to start recruiting faculty and students without accreditation.

Since none of us had any experience in establishing a university, we relied on energetic and entrepreneurial academics to set up individual departments. CEU is perhaps the only modern university created by those who would be teaching in it; as a result, we had functioning departments even before the university was established. The renowned Hungarian historian Peter Hanák started a department of modern comparative history. The even more highly respected medieval historian, Gabor Klaniczay, set up a department of medieval history that became famous for studying the major medieval religions and their interactions: Byzantine and Latin Christianity, Judaism and Islam. András Sajó, a constitutional scholar who later became vice president of the European Court of Human Rights, together with George Fletcher, a scholar of criminal law from Columbia University, started a legal studies program, focusing on the timely issues of constitutionalism and transitional justice. The famous social anthropologist Ernest Gellner, a close friend of Karl Popper, launched a program in nationalism studies. Not bad for a fledgling university!

We were inundated with luminaries and experts who came to give lectures and short courses. Against the odds, CEU opened its doors in Prague in September 1991. Karl Popper visited the remnants of the Prague campus in 1994, and I was there to give him the first CEU "Open Society Prize."

Our Luxembourg solution did not stand the test of time, and we needed to find proper accreditation. Our ever-ingenious Paul Flather looked to the United States and found that the State of New York did not require a university recognized by it to be physically located within the state. This is how the famous American University in Beirut has been operating for more than one and a half centuries. We applied to the New York Board of Regents, and they accepted our application. That was the beginning of CEU's association with Leon Botstein, president of Bard College, who steered us through the bureaucracy of the New York Board of Regents. He later became and is still the chairman of CEU's board.

In the first years of its existence, CEU operated in three locations: some of the departments (economics, European studies, international relations, nationalism studies, art history) were located in Prague, where Jiri Musil, an urban sociologist and one of Václav Havel's advisors, was director of the college. History, medieval studies, political science, environmental sciences, legal and gender studies, and, later on, philosophy and mathematics were located in Budapest, where the historian István Rév was the director. He also established the Open Society Archives, containing the richest collection of *samizdat* publications. CEU set up its sociology program in Warsaw, in cooperation with the Graduate School of Social Research of the Polish Academy of Sciences.

In the early 1990s, we set up an environmental program in Budapest under the leadership of Sir Richard Southwood, vice chancellor of Oxford, who was an authority on ecology, radiation hazards, and pollution control. It became one of the leading teaching programs in this field, much sought after by students. Gradually all the departments gravitated toward Budapest.

The existence of independent departments created untold problems later, when the university was properly established. The first de facto president, Bill Newton-Smith, had to grapple with the idiosyncratic ways of each department: different entrance requirements, individual examination styles, and even their own term-time dates.

Subsequent presidents had to overcome the resistance of entrenched department heads.

Also on the negative side, Newton-Smith failed to meet my requirement for matching funds. It was not his fault. In 1992, I became known as "the man who broke the Bank of England." After this, nobody would give money to CEU. A man who made more than a billion dollars in a day could surely afford to pay for it himself. I had to accept this fact and became the sole funder after all. Moreover, my principles eventually obliged me to give the CEU a large endowment in order to assure its independence from me. This took care of the bulk of the money that I had made from "breaking the Bank of England."

The CEU Board appointed Yehuda Elkana as president and rector in 1999. His ten-year tenure marked a significant transformation of the university. Born in Hungary, Elkana was a Holocaust survivor who became a leader of the peace movement in Israel. He was an iconoclast thinker, scholar, and educator. He was also a visionary leader. Deeply committed to the open society mission of CEU, he also believed that no university can deserve its name unless it does serious research. In a few years he transformed CEU into a mission-driven but also research-intensive university. He convinced me that CEU should gradually go global rather than remain confined exclusively to Central and Eastern Europe. He was the first to come up with the idea that CEU is too small and isolated to survive and flourish alone and that it would need to network globally to overcome this handicap.

Today, CEU enrolls students from over one hundred countries.

In our last meeting in 2009 I asked him what more I could do to help CEU. His answer was that I should step down as chairman of the Board and double the endowment. I am doing as he advised. By enlarging CEU's endowment, I will ensure its financial stability, academic excellence, and global reach. I expect it to play a key role in innovation in higher education through the creation of links among institutions across borders and the protection of academic freedom for scholars and students worldwide.

——————

My goal was to create a university that takes its principles and its social responsibilities seriously.

CEU became that university. As I invested increasing amounts in CEU, I also invested equal amounts in a Higher Education Support Program (HESP). CEU was draining the best talent from the existing educational system; the task of HESP was to replace the talent. When my annual support to CEU reached $20 million, I fixed my annual contribution to HESP at that level.

HESP had its own board, and at first it was managed independently from CEU, but of course, the two of them cooperated. Gradually, the separation became blurred, and eventually the two of them practically merged. By then, CEU had done enough for the state systems—mainly by

educating professors who worked in the state systems—
that they didn't need HESP to sustain them. HESP became
focused on the development of higher education, including
curricular development, faculty mobility, summer schools,
and the autonomy and management of universities.

———

The participants of the 1989 Dubrovnik seminar advocated
for a new university that would take the medieval university of Bologna as its model. The original Bologna University was a multinational, multiethnic school where the
students, coming mostly from the countries of Southern
and Eastern Europe, studied together; they had a common
language, not only in the sense that they all understood
Latin but also in the sense that they could understand each
other. Bologna educated a regional elite who could talk to
each other because they knew each other.

The founding years of CEU coincided with the out-
break of the Yugoslav wars. Students from Yugoslavia
found themselves stranded all over Europe, separated from
their families and without financial resources. We gave
them scholarships to come to CEU. At a moment when
Serbs and Croats ceased to talk to each other in Serbo-
Croatian, pretending that they spoke different languages,
the students at CEU kept talking to each other in today's
lingua franca, English, the language of instruction at CEU.
Despite the vicious armed conflicts and the genocide in

Srebrenica, CEU did not witness a single incident of physical violence.

We had Chechen and Russian students, Israelis and Palestinians, Afghans and Americans, Chinese and Taiwanese. They differed, disagreed, argued—but kept talking to each other. Living and studying together, arguing with each other, and learning to think critically helped them to listen to each other and remain engaged.

————

CEU has been a great success. It has graduated sixteen thousand students from all parts of the world. For many of them, CEU was the only chance to get access to graduate education. When they return home, they often assume leadership positions in developing democracies. This is what I am most proud of.

CEU has steadfastly defended the principle of academic freedom over the years and, more recently, fought back against a concerted attack by Prime Minister Viktor Orbán, who deployed all the powers of his "mafia state" to destroy the entire higher education system of Hungary and chase away CEU. Its epic struggle against a repressive regime, led by its current rector, the eminent Canadian public intellectual Michael Ignatieff, generated worldwide support. That struggle is still ongoing.

CEU has been forced to move its US accredited degree-giving courses to Vienna. However, it intends to maintain a presence in Budapest. The faculty and students of numerous universities, as well as many ordinary Hungarian citizens, repeatedly took to the streets to demonstrate in solidarity with CEU. CEU feels morally obliged to reciprocate.

Keeping two campuses and moving to Vienna, where the cost of living is much higher, will almost double the cost of maintaining the university. At the same time, CEU must compete for faculty and students with state-owned universities, which are subsidized by the state and charge reduced or no tuition fees. The Open Society Foundations support CEU, but they also need to meet many other urgent demands and, in any case, their resources are insignificant in comparison with those of entire states. That has created a seemingly insoluble problem.

We can survive only if we can offer something outstanding and perhaps unique that can attract funding not only from the Open Society Foundations but also from other sources. We are already among the hundred best universities of the world in the social sciences and humanities, and we are one of the largest recipients of research grants from the European Union in the fields in which we operate. But we must aim even higher.

The only solution is to turn CEU into something unique: a globally networked university that meets the requirements of the twenty-first century. That will deserve the support of many donors in addition to the Open Society Foundations.

We already have the necessary building blocks; all we need is to put them together. CEU, which is a graduate and postgraduate university, already has a close collaboration with Bard College, which is mainly undergraduate. Both have been supported by the Open Society Foundation (OSF) and cooperated with each other for more than two decades; we need to turn this into a binding cooperation agreement. Both Bard and CEU have a network of associated colleges, universities, and other institutions, and the two lists are largely overlapping. The combination of an undergraduate education based largely on Bard and a postgraduate education and lifelong learning built on CEU ought to be very rewarding.

American students are used to donating to their alma mater. Having a unique, global education and having it entirely within the CEU-Bard network should eventually make it largely self-financing. Other donors, in turn, should find this reassuring.

The CEU's New York campus, which is currently at a rudimentary stage, also needs developing in order to provide donors an opportunity to get to know CEU better. But Open Society Foundations cannot divert its much sought-after resources to that purpose, the expansion of the New York campus has to be donor financed from inception.

Our task is to develop a global Open Society University Network (OSUN) that will be open to institutions that don't belong to the existing CEU-Bard network but express an interest in joining it. This impressive network will be composed of progressive and well-recognized universities all over the world. We already have nodes in the US (New York and California) and Europe (Berlin, Vienna, and Budapest), as well as in Russia (St. Petersburg and Moscow), Central Asia (Bishkek), the Middle East (Al-Quds in East Jerusalem), and East Asia (China, Myanmar, and Vietnam). Bard College has also extended the reach of higher education to prisons and early colleges.

I am particularly keen to develop the already existing cooperation with Arizona State University (ASU). ASU is a leading institution in online and blended education and, more broadly, in increasing access to higher education. This is of great interest for OSUN, which plans to develop as a globally networked university. ASU's current leadership also shares our idea of social responsibility and is ready to help us in developing distance and blended learning, in which CEU and Bard are less advanced. Blended learning combines the use of online and electronic media with face-to-face mentoring.

OSUN will be something genuinely innovative and unique. Many first-tier American universities have established academic colonies overseas (e.g., New York University in Abu Dhabi) where the overseas colony is intended to support the mission and, often, the bottom line of the founding institution. OSUN will be a partnership of equals established for mutual benefit. It will be the world's first truly global university, and it will offer an alternative model of international cooperation.

After the lifetime of its founder, OSUN will be renamed the Soros University Network. It is an ambitious project. But if anybody is able to turn OSUN into reality, it is CEU-Bard in its new incarnation. It will meet the requirements of a twenty-first-century globally networked university and, at the same time, help open societies to confront their enemies—provided it can mobilize sufficient support.

CHAPTER 4

The Global Financial Crisis and Its Aftermath

"A Better Bailout Was Possible"

(Excerpt from *The Crash of 2008 and What It Means*, written almost contemporaneously and published in 2009.)

The Crash of 2008

The bankruptcy of Lehman Brothers on Monday, September 15, 2008, was a game-changing event. Until then, whenever the financial system came close to a breakdown, the authorities intervened. This time they did not. The consequences were disastrous. CDSs (credit default swaps) went through the roof, and American International Group (AIG), which carried a large short position in CDSs, was facing imminent default. By the next day, Tuesday, Treasury Secretary Henry Paulson had to reverse himself and come to the rescue of AIG, albeit on extremely punitive terms. But worse was to come. Lehman was one of the main market makers in commercial paper and a major issuer. An independent money market fund held Lehman paper, and since it had no deep pocket to turn to, it had to "break the buck"—stop redeeming its shares at par. This caused panic among depositors, and by Thursday, a run on money market funds was in full swing. The panic spread to the stock market. The Federal Reserve had to extend a guarantee to all money market funds, short selling of financial stocks was suspended, and the Treasury announced a $700 billion rescue package for the banking system. This provided some temporary relief to the stock market.

Paulson's $700 billion rescue package was ill-conceived; more exactly, it was not conceived at all. Strange as it is, the Treasury secretary was simply not prepared for the consequences of his action when he allowed Lehman

Brothers to fail. When the financial system collapsed, he had to rush to Congress without any clear idea of how he was going to use the money he was asking for and only a rudimentary concept of setting up something like the Resolution Trust Corporation, which acquired and eventually disposed of the assets of failing savings-and-loan institutions in the savings-and-loan crisis of the 1980s. So he asked for total discretion, including immunity from legal challenge. Unsurprisingly, Congress did not give it to him. Several voices, my own included, argued convincingly that the money would be better spent injecting equity into banks rather than taking toxic assets off their hands. Eventually, Secretary Paulson came around to the idea, but he did not execute it properly. I outlined how it should have been done in an article published in the *Financial Times* on September 24, 2008.

Conditions in the financial system continued to deteriorate. The commercial paper market ground to a halt, LIBOR (the London interbank offered rate) rose, swap spreads widened, CDSs blew out, and investment banks and other financial institutions without direct access to the Federal Reserve could not get overnight or short-term credit. The Fed had to extend one lifeline after another. It was in this atmosphere that the International Monetary Fund (IMF) held its annual meeting in Washington, starting on October 11, 2008. The European leaders left early and met in Paris on Sunday, October 12. At that meeting, they decided to, in effect, guarantee that no major European financial institution would be allowed to fail. They could not agree, however, to do it on an inclusive Europe-wide basis, so each country set up its own arrangements. The United States followed suit in short order.

These arrangements had an unintended adverse side effect all over the world: they brought additional pressure to bear on the countries that could not extend similarly credible guarantees to their financial institutions. Iceland was already in a state of collapse. The largest bank in Hungary was now subjected to a bear raid, and the currencies and government bond markets of Hungary and the other Eastern European countries fell precipitously. The same happened to Brazil, Mexico, the Asian tigers, and, to a lesser extent, Turkey, South Africa, China, India, Australia, and New Zealand. The euro tanked and the yen soared. The dollar strengthened on a trade-weighted basis. Trade credit in the periphery countries dried up. The precipitous currency moves claimed some victims. Leading exporters in Brazil had gotten into the habit of selling options against their appreciating currency and now became insolvent, precipitating a local mini-crash.

All these dislocations taken together had a tremendous impact on the behavior and attitudes of consumers, businesses, and financial institutions throughout the world. The financial system had been in crisis since August 2007, but the general public hardly noticed it and, with some exceptions, business carried on as usual. All this changed in the weeks following September 15, 2008. The global economy fell off a cliff, and this became evident as the statistics for October and November began to appear. The wealth effect was enormous. Pension funds, university endowments, and charitable institutions lost anywhere between 20 and 40 percent of their assets within a couple of months—and that was before the $50 billion Bernard Madoff scandal was exposed. The self-reinforcing recognition that we are facing a deep and long recession, possibly amounting to a depression, has become widespread.

The Federal Reserve responded forcefully, slashing the Fed fund rate to practically zero on December 16, 2008, and embarking on quantitative easing. The Obama administration is preparing a two-year fiscal stimulus package in the $850 billion range and other radical measures.

The international response has been more muted. The IMF has approved a new facility that allows periphery countries in sound financial condition to borrow up to five times their quota without conditionality, but the amounts are puny, and the possibility of a stigma continues to linger. As a result, the facility remains unused. The Fed opened swap lines with Mexico, Brazil, Korea, and Singapore. But European Central Bank president Jean-Claude Trichet inveighed against fiscal irresponsibility, and Germany remains adamantly opposed to excessive money creation that may lay the groundwork for inflationary pressures in the future. These divergent attitudes render concerted international action extremely difficult to achieve. They may also cause wide swings in exchange rates.

In retrospect, the bankruptcy of Lehman Brothers is comparable to the bank failures that occurred in the 1930s.

How could it have been allowed to occur? The responsibility lies squarely with the financial authorities, notably the Treasury and the Federal Reserve. They claim that they lacked the necessary legal powers, but that is a lame excuse. In an emergency, they could and should have done whatever was necessary to prevent the system from collapsing. That is what they have done on other occasions. The fact is that they allowed it to happen. Why?

I would draw a distinction between Treasury Secretary Paulson and Federal Reserve Chairman Ben Bernanke. Paulson was in charge because Lehman Brothers, as an investment bank, was not under the aegis of the Federal Reserve. In my view, Paulson was reluctant to resort to the use of "taxpayers' money" because he knew that it would entail increased government control. He was a true market fundamentalist. He believed that the same methods and instruments that got the markets into trouble could be used to get them out of it. This led to his abortive plan to create a super-SIV (special investment vehicle) to take over failing SIVs. He subscribed to the doctrine that markets have greater powers to adjust than any individual participant. Coming six months after the Bear Stearns crisis, he must have thought that markets had had enough notice to prepare for the failure of Lehman Brothers. That is why he had no Plan B when the markets broke down.

Ben Bernanke was less of an ideologue, but coming from an academic background, the bursting of the super-bubble found him unprepared. Originally, he asserted that the housing bubble was an isolated phenomenon that could cause losses up to $100 billion, which could be easily absorbed. He did not realize that equilibrium theory was fundamentally flawed; as a consequence, he could not anticipate that the various methods and instruments based on the false assumption that prices deviate from a theoretical equilibrium in a random manner would fail one after another in short order. But he was a fast learner. When he saw it happening, he responded by drastically lowering interest rates, first in January 2008 and again in December. Unfortunately, his learning process started too late and always lagged behind the actual course of events. That is how the situation spun out of control.

On a deeper level, the demise of Lehman Brothers conclusively falsifies the efficient market hypothesis. My argument is bound to be controversial, but it raises some very interesting questions. Each of its three steps will take the reader to unfamiliar grounds.

The first step is to acknowledge that there is an asymmetry between being long or short in the stock market. (Being long means owning a stock; being short means selling a stock one does not own.) Going long has unlimited potential on the upside but limited exposure on the downside, being short is the reverse. The asymmetry manifests itself in the following way: losing on a long position reduces one's risk exposure, while losing on a short position increases it. As a result, one can be more patient being long and wrong than being short and wrong. The asymmetry serves to discourage the short selling of stocks.

The second step is to understand CDSs and to recognize that the CDS market offers a convenient way of shorting bonds. In that market the risk-reward asymmetry works in the opposite way to stocks. Going short on bonds by buying a CDS contract carries limited risk but unlimited profit potential; by contrast, selling CDSs offers limited profits but practically unlimited risks. The asymmetry encourages speculating on the short side, which in turn exerts a downward pressure on the underlying bonds. When an adverse development is expected, the negative effect can become overwhelming because CDSs tend to be priced as warrants, not as options: people buy them not because they expect an eventual default but because they expect the CDSs to appreciate in case of adverse developments. No arbitrage can correct the mispricing. That can be clearly seen in the case of US and UK government bonds: the actual price of the bonds is much higher than the price implied by CDSs. These asymmetries are difficult to reconcile with the efficient market hypothesis.

The third step is to take into account reflexivity and recognize that the mispricing of financial instruments can affect the fundamentals that market prices are supposed to reflect. Nowhere is this phenomenon more pronounced than in the case of financial institutions, whose ability to do business is so dependent on confidence and trust. A decline in their share and bond prices can increase their financing costs. That means that bear raids on financial institutions can be self-validating, which is in direct contradiction to the efficient market hypothesis.

Putting these three considerations together leads to the conclusion that Lehman Brothers, AIG, and other financial institutions were destroyed by bear raids in which the shorting of stocks and buying of CDSs mutually amplified and reinforced each other. The unlimited shorting of stocks was made possible by the abolition of the uptick rule, which would have hindered bear raids by allowing short selling only when prices were rising. The unlimited shorting of bonds was facilitated by the CDS market. The two together made a lethal combination. That is what AIG, one of the most successful insurance companies in the world, failed to understand. Its business was selling insurance, and when it saw a seriously mispriced risk, it went to town insuring it in the belief that diversifying risk reduces it. It expected to make a fortune in the long run, but it was destroyed in the short run because it did not realize that it was selling not insurance but warrants for shorting bonds.

My argument lends itself to empirical research. The evidence shows that the CDS market is much larger than all the bond markets put together—having peaked at an amazing $62 trillion nominal amount outstanding. There is only anecdotal evidence that there was some collusion between the people who shorted stocks and bought CDSs, but the matter could be further investigated. The prima facie evidence favors the conclusion.

This raises some interesting questions: What would have happened if the uptick rule had been kept in effect and speculating in CDSs had been outlawed? The bankruptcy of Lehman Brothers might have been avoided, but what would have happened to the super-bubble? One can only conjecture. My guess is that the super-bubble would have been deflated more slowly, with less catastrophic results, but the aftereffects would have lingered longer. It would have resembled the Japanese experience more than what is happening now.

What is the proper role of short selling? Undoubtedly, it gives markets greater depth and continuity, making them more resilient, but it is not without dangers. Bear raids can be self-validating and ought to be kept under control. If the efficient market hypothesis were valid, there would be an *a priori* reason for not imposing any constraints. As it is, both the uptick rule and allowing short selling only when it is covered by actually borrowed stock are useful pragmatic measures that seem to work well without any clear-cut theoretical justification.

What about credit default swaps? Here I take a more radical view than most people. The prevailing view is that they ought to be traded on regulated exchanges. I believe they are toxic and should be used only by prescription. They could be allowed to be used to insure actual bonds but—in light of their asymmetric character—not to speculate against countries or companies.* CDSs are not

---

*Trading in CDSs is creating trouble for the euro. Several countries within the Euroblock are getting over-indebted and facing the prospect of being downgraded by the rating agencies. The buying of CDS contracts puts additional pressure on their borrowing costs and diminishes the benefit of being members of the

the only synthetic financial instruments that have proven toxic. The same applies to the slicing and dicing of CDOs (collateralized debt obligations) and to the portfolio insurance contracts that caused the stock market crash of 1987, to mention only two instruments that have actually done a lot of damage. The issuance of stock is closely regulated by the SEC—why not the issuance of derivatives and other synthetic instruments? Most importantly, the role of reflexivity and the asymmetries I have identified ought to prompt a rejection of the efficient market hypothesis and a thorough reconsideration of the regulatory regime.

Now that the bankruptcy of Lehman Brothers has had the same shock effect on the behavior of consumers and businesses as the bank failures of the 1930s, the problems facing the Obama administration are at least twice as great as those that confronted President Franklin Roosevelt. This can be seen from a simple calculation. Total credit outstanding was 160 percent of GDP in 1929, and it rose to 260 percent in 1932 due to the accumulation of debt and the decline of GDP. We entered into the crash of 2008 at 365 percent, which is bound to rise to 500 percent or more by the time the full effect is felt. And this calculation does not take into account the pervasive use of derivatives, which was absent in the 1930s but immensely complicates the current situation.

Euroblock. This casts doubts on the durability of the euro. There is an independently existing underlying weakness in the euro, which is exacerbated by the CDS market in a self-reinforcing fashion.

The nominal amount of CDS contracts outstanding is more than four times the GDP. On the positive side, we have the experience of the 1930s and the prescriptions of John Maynard Keynes to draw on. His *General Theory of Employment, Interest, and Money* was published only in 1936; we have it at our disposal from the outset.

Paulson Cannot Be Allowed a Blank Check

(Article published in the *Financial Times* on September 24, 2008.)

Hank Paulson's $700 billion rescue package has run into difficulty on Capitol Hill. Rightly so: it was ill-conceived. Congress would be abdicating its responsibility if it gave the Treasury secretary a blank check. The bill submitted to Congress even had language in it that would exempt the secretary's decisions from review by any court or administrative agency—the ultimate fulfillment of the Bush administration's dream of a unitary executive.

Mr. Paulson's record does not inspire the confidence necessary to give him discretion over $700 billion. His actions last week brought on the crisis that makes rescue necessary. On Monday, he allowed Lehman Brothers to fail and refused to make government funds available to save AIG. By Tuesday, he had to reverse himself and provide an $85 billion loan to AIG on punitive terms. The demise of Lehman disrupted the commercial paper market. A large money market fund "broke the buck," and investment banks that relied on the commercial paper market had difficulty financing their operations. By Thursday, a run on money market funds was in full swing, and we came as close to a meltdown as at any time since the 1930s. Mr. Paulson reversed again and proposed a systemic rescue.

Mr. Paulson had gotten a blank check from Congress once before. That was to deal with Fannie Mae and

Freddie Mac. His solution landed the housing market in the worst of all worlds: their managements knew that if the blank checks were filled out, they would lose their jobs, so they retrenched and made mortgages more expensive and less available. Within a few weeks, the market forced Mr. Paulson's hand and he had to take them over.

Mr. Paulson's proposal to purchase distressed mortgage-related securities poses a classic problem of asymmetric information. The securities are hard to value, but the sellers know more about them than the buyer: in any auction process, the Treasury would end up with the dregs. The proposal is also rife with latent conflict-of-interest issues. Unless the Treasury overpays for the securities, the scheme would not bring relief. But if the scheme is used to bail out insolvent banks, what will the taxpayers get in return?

Barack Obama has outlined four conditions that ought to be imposed: an upside for the taxpayers as well as a downside, a bipartisan board to oversee the process, help for the homeowners as well as the holders of the mortgages, and some limits on the compensation of those who benefit from taxpayers' money. These are the right principles. They could be applied more effectively by capitalizing the institutions that are burdened by distressed securities directly rather than by relieving them of the distressed securities.

The injection of government funds would be much less problematic if it were applied to the equity rather than to the balance sheet. $700 billion in preferred stock with warrants may be sufficient to make up the hole created by the bursting of the housing bubble. By contrast, the addition of $700 billion on the demand side of an $11,000 billion market may not be sufficient to arrest the decline of housing prices.

Something also needs to be done on the supply side. To prevent housing prices from overshooting on the downside, the number of foreclosures has to be kept to a minimum. The terms of mortgages need to be adjusted to the homeowners' ability to pay.

The rescue package leaves this task undone. Making the necessary modifications is a delicate task rendered more difficult by the fact that many mortgages have been sliced up and repackaged in the form of collateralized debt obligations. The holders of the various slices have conflicting interests. It would take too long to work out the conflicts to include a mortgage modification scheme in the rescue package. The package can, however, prepare the ground by modifying bankruptcy law as it relates to principal residences.

Now that the crisis has been unleashed, a large-scale rescue package is probably indispensable to bring it under control. Rebuilding the depleted balance sheets of the banking system is the right way to go. Not every bank deserves to be saved, but the experts at the Federal Reserve, with proper supervision, can be counted on to make the right judgments. Managements that are reluctant to accept the consequences of past mistakes could be penalized by depriving them of the Fed's credit facilities. Making government funds available should also encourage the private sector to participate in recapitalizing the banking sector and bringing the financial crisis to a close.

A Better Bailout Was Possible

(Article cowritten with Rob Johnson,
published on *Project Syndicate* on September 18, 2018.)

The recent exchange between Joe Stiglitz and Larry Summers about "secular stagnation" and its relation to the tepid economic recovery after the 2008–2009 financial crisis is an important one. Stiglitz and Summers appear to agree that policy was inadequate to address the structural challenges that the crisis revealed and intensified. Their debate addresses the size of the fiscal stimulus, the role of financial regulation, and the importance of income distribution. But additional issues need to be explored in depth.

We believe a critical opportunity was missed when the balance of the burden of adjustment was tilted heavily in favor of creditors relative to debtors in the response to the crisis and that this contributed to the prolonged stagnation that followed the crisis. The long-term social and political ramifications of this missed opportunity have been profound.

Back in September 2008, when then US Secretary of the Treasury Hank Paulson introduced the $700 billion Troubled Asset Relief Program (TARP), he proposed using the funds to bail out the banks but without acquiring any equity ownership in them. At that time, we and our colleague Robert Dugger argued that a much more effective and fair use of taxpayers' money would be to reduce the value of mortgages held by ordinary Americans to reflect the decline in home prices and to inject capital into the financial institutions that would become under-capitalized. Because equity could support a balance sheet that would have been twenty times larger, $700 billion could have gone a long way toward restoring a healthy financial system.

The ability to use funds to inject equity into the banks was not part of the bill presented to the US House of Representatives. So we organized for Representative Jim Moran to ask House Financial Services chairman Barney Frank in a prearranged question whether it was in the spirit of the TARP legislation to allow the Treasury to use taxpayers' money in the form of equity injections. Frank replied in the affirmative on the House floor.

This was in fact a tool that Paulson used in the closing days of George W. Bush's administration. But Paulson did it the wrong way: he summoned the heads of major banks and forced them to take the money he allocated to them. But by doing so, he stigmatized the banks.

A few months later, when President Barack Obama's administration arrived, one of us (Soros) repeatedly appealed to Summers to adopt a policy of equity injection into fragile financial institutions and to write down mortgages to a realistic market value in order to help the economy recover. Summers objected that this would be politically unacceptable because it would mean nationalizing banks. Such a policy reeked of socialism and America is not a socialist country, he asserted.

We found his argument unconvincing—both then and now. By relieving financial institutions of their overvalued assets, the Bush and Obama administrations had already chosen to socialize the downside. Only the upside of sharing in the possible stock gains in the event of a recovery was still at issue!

Had our policy recommendation been adopted, stockholders and debt holders (who have a higher propensity to save) would have experienced greater losses than they did, whereas lower- and middle-income households (which have a higher propensity to consume) would have experienced relief from their mortgage debt. This shift in the burden of adjustment would have imposed losses on the people who were responsible for the calamity, stimulated aggregate demand, and diminished the rising inequality that was demoralizing the vast majority of people.

We did recognize a problem with our proposal: providing relief to overindebted mortgage holders would have encountered resistance from the many homeowners who had not taken out a mortgage. We were exploring ways to overcome this problem until it became moot: the Obama administration refused to accept our advice.

The approach of the Bush and Obama administrations stands in stark contrast both to the policy followed by the British government and to earlier examples of successful financial bailouts in the United States.

In Great Britain, led by then Prime Minister Gordon Brown, undercapitalized banks were told to raise additional capital. They were given the opportunity to go to the market themselves, but they were warned that the UK Treasury would inject funds into them if they failed to do so. The Royal Bank of Scotland and Lloyds TSB did require government support. The equity injections were accompanied by restrictions on executive pay and dividends. In contrast to Paulson's method of injecting funds, banks were not stigmatized if they could borrow from the markets.

Similarly, during the Great Depression of the 1930s, the United States took ownership and recapitalized banks via the Reconstruction Finance Corporation (RFC) and managed mortgage restructuring through the Home Owners' Loan Corporation (HOLC).

No doubt the Obama administration helped to alleviate the crisis by reassuring the public and downplaying the depth of the problems, but there was a heavy political price to pay. The administration's policies failed to deal with the underlying problems, and by protecting the banks rather than mortgage holders, they exacerbated the gap between America's haves and have-nots.

The electorate blamed the Obama administration and the Democratic Congress for the results. The Tea Party was formed in early 2009 with large-scale financial support from the billionaire Koch brothers, Charles and David. In January 2010, Massachusetts held a special election for the late Ted Kennedy's Senate seat, just after Wall Street paid extravagant bonuses, and elected the Republican Scott Brown. The Republicans subsequently took control of the

House of Representatives in the 2010 midterm elections, gained control of the Senate in 2014, and nominated Donald Trump, who was elected in 2016.

It is essential that the Democratic Party recognize and correct its past mistakes. The 2018 midterm elections, which will set the stage for the 2020 presidential election, are an excellent opportunity to do so. The political and economic problems that confront the country are much deeper today than they were ten years ago, and the public knows it.

The Democrats must recognize these problems, not downplay them. This year's midterm elections will be a plebiscite on Trump, but the Democratic presidential candidate in 2020 must have a program that many Americans find inspiring. The electorate has seen where the Republicans' demagogic populism leads, and a majority should reject it in 2018.

CHAPTER 5

The Tragedy of the European Union

"Europe, Please Wake Up!"

"Wake Up, Europe"

(Excerpts from "Wake Up, Europe," published in the
New York Review of Books on October 22, 2014.)

Europe is facing a challenge from Russia. Neither the European leaders nor their citizens are fully aware of this challenge or know how best to deal with it. Russia has adopted the use of force that manifests itself in repression at home and aggression abroad, as opposed to the rule of law. What is shocking is that Vladimir Putin's Russia has proved to be in some ways superior to the European Union—more flexible and constantly springing surprises. That has given it a tactical advantage, at least in the near term.

Europe and the United States—each for its own reasons—are determined to avoid any direct military confrontation with Russia. Russia is taking advantage of their reluctance. Violating its treaty obligations, Russia has annexed Crimea and established separatist enclaves in eastern Ukraine. In 2014, when the recently installed government in Kiev threatened to win the low-level war in eastern Ukraine against separatist forces backed by Russia, President Putin invaded Ukraine with regular armed forces disguised as "little green men." This violated Russian law that protects conscripts from being deployed abroad without their consent.

In seventy-two hours, these forces destroyed several hundred of Ukraine's armored vehicles, a substantial portion of its fighting force. According to General Wesley

Clark, former NATO supreme allied commander for Europe, the Russians used multiple-launch rocket systems armed with cluster munitions and thermal-baric warheads (an even more inhumane weapon that ought to be outlawed), with devastating effect. The local militia from the Ukrainian city of Dnepropetrovsk suffered the brunt of the losses because they were communicating by cell phones and could thus easily be located and targeted by the Russians. President Putin has, so far, abided by a ceasefire agreement he concluded with Ukrainian president Petro Poroshenko on September 5, 2014, but Putin retains the choice to continue the ceasefire as long as he finds it advantageous or to resume a full-scale assault.

In September 2014, President Poroshenko visited Washington, where he received an enthusiastic welcome from a joint session of Congress. He asked for "both lethal and nonlethal" defensive weapons in his speech. However, President Obama refused his request for Javelin handheld missiles that could be used against advancing tanks. Poroshenko was given radar, but what use was it without missiles? European countries were equally reluctant to provide military assistance to Ukraine, fearing Russian retaliation. The Washington visit gave President Poroshenko a façade of support with little substance behind it.

The collapse of Ukraine would be a tremendous loss for NATO, the European Union, and the United States. A victorious Russia would become much more influential within the EU and pose a potent threat to the Baltic states, with their large ethnic Russian populations. Instead of supporting Ukraine, NATO would have to defend itself on its own soil. This would expose both the European Union and the United States to the danger they have been so eager to avoid: a direct military confrontation with Russia. The European Union would become even more divided and ungovernable. Why should the United States and other NATO nations allow this to happen?

The argument that has prevailed in both Europe and the United States is that Putin is no Hitler; by giving him everything he can reasonably ask for, he can be prevented from resorting to further use of force. In the meantime, the sanctions against Russia—which include, for example, restrictions on business transactions, finance, and trade—will have their effect, and in the long run, Russia will have to retreat in order to earn some relief from them.

These are false hopes derived from a false argument with no factual evidence to support it. Putin has repeatedly resorted to force and is liable to do so again unless he faces strong resistance. Even if it is possible that the hypothesis could turn out to be valid, it is extremely irresponsible not to prepare a Plan B.

There are two counterarguments that are less obvious but even more important. First, Western authorities have ignored the importance of what I call the "new Ukraine" that was born in the successful resistance on the Maidan. Many officials with a history of dealing with Ukraine have difficulty adjusting to the revolutionary change that has taken place there. The recently signed Association Agreement between the EU and Ukraine was originally negotiated with the Viktor Yanukovych government. This detailed road map now needs adjustment to a totally different reality. For instance, the road map calls for the gradual replacement and retraining of the judiciary over five years, whereas the public is clamoring for immediate and radical renewal. As the mayor of Kiev, Vitali Klitschko, put it, "If you put fresh cucumbers into a barrel of pickles, they will soon turn into pickles."

Contrary to some widely circulated accounts, the resistance on the Maidan was led by the cream of civil society: young people, many of whom had studied abroad and refused to join either government or business on their return because they found both of them repugnant. (Nationalists and anti-Semitic extremists made up only a small minority of the anti-Yanukovych protesters.) They are the leaders of the new Ukraine, and they are adamantly opposed to a return of the "old Ukraine," with its endemic corruption and ineffective government.

The new Ukraine has to contend with Russian aggression, bureaucratic resistance both at home and abroad, and confusion in the general population. Surprisingly, it has had the support of several oligarchs, former President Poroshenko foremost among them. There are, of course, profound differences in history, language, and outlook between the eastern and western parts of the country, but Ukraine is more united and more European-minded than ever before. That unity, however, is extremely fragile.

The new Ukraine has remained largely unrecognized because it took time before it could make its influence felt.

It had practically no trained security forces at its disposal when it was born. The security forces of the old Ukraine were actively engaged in suppressing the Maidan rebellion and were disoriented this summer when they had to take orders from a government formed by the supporters of the rebellion. No wonder the new government was at first unable to put up an effective resistance to the establishment of the separatist enclaves in eastern Ukraine. It is all the more remarkable that then President Poroshenko was able, within a few months of his election, to mount an attack that threatened to reclaim those enclaves.

To appreciate the merits of the new Ukraine, you need to have had some personal experience with it. I can speak from personal experience, although I must also confess to a bias in its favor. I established a foundation in Ukraine in 1990, even before the country became independent. Its board and staff are composed entirely of Ukrainians, and it has deep roots in civil society. I visited the country often, especially in the early years, but not between 2004 and early 2014, when I returned to witness the birth of the new Ukraine.

I was immediately impressed by the tremendous improvement in maturity and expertise during that time both in my foundation and in civil society at large. Currently, civic and political engagement is probably higher than anywhere else in Europe. People have proven their willingness to sacrifice their lives for their country. These are the hidden strengths of the new Ukraine that have been overlooked by the West.

The other deficiency of the current European attitude toward Ukraine is that it fails to recognize that the Russian attack on Ukraine is indirectly an attack on the European Union and its principles of governance. It ought to be evident that it is inappropriate for a country, or association of countries, at war to pursue a policy of fiscal austerity as the European Union continues to do. All available resources ought to be put to work in the war effort, even if that involves running up budget deficits. The fragility of the new Ukraine makes the ambivalence of the West all the more perilous. Not only the survival of the new Ukraine but also the future of NATO and the European Union itself is at risk. In the absence of unified resistance, it is unrealistic to expect that Putin will stop pushing beyond Ukraine when the division of Europe and its domination by Russia is in sight.

Having identified some of the shortcomings of the current approach, I will try to spell out the course that Europe ought to follow. Sanctions against Russia are necessary, but they are a necessary evil. They have a depressive effect not only on Russia but also on the European economies, including Germany. This aggravates the recessionary and deflationary forces that are already at work. By contrast, assisting Ukraine in defending itself against Russian aggression would have a stimulative effect not only on Ukraine but also on Europe. That is the principle that ought to guide European assistance to Ukraine.

The new Ukraine has the political will both to defend Europe against Russian aggression and to engage in radical structural reforms. To preserve and reinforce that will, Ukraine needs to receive adequate assistance from its supporters. Without it, the results will be disappointing and hope will turn into despair.

It is high time for the members of the European Union to wake up and behave as countries indirectly at war. They are better off helping Ukraine to defend itself than having to fight for themselves. One way or another, the internal contradiction between being at war and remaining committed to fiscal austerity has to be eliminated. Where there is a will, there is a way.

It is also high time for the European Union to take a critical look at itself. There must be something wrong with the EU if Putin's Russia can be so successful, even in the short term. The bureaucracy of the EU no longer has a monopoly on power, and it has little to be proud of. It should learn to be more united, flexible, and efficient. And Europeans themselves need to take a close look at the new Ukraine. That could help them recapture the original spirit that led to the creation of the European Union. The European Union would save itself by saving Ukraine.

What Went Wrong and How to Fix It

(Remarks delivered at the Brussels Economic Forum
on June 1, 2017.)

I should like to dedicate my remarks to the memory of my
great friend Tommaso Padoa Schioppa. My purpose today
is to explain what Tommaso Padoa Schioppa and I would
be working on together if he were still alive.

We would try to save the European Union in order to
radically reinvent it. The first objective, saving Europe,
has to take precedence because it is in existential danger.
But we wouldn't forget about the second objective either.

The reinvention would have to revive the support that
the European Union used to enjoy. We would do it by
reviewing the past and explaining what went wrong and
how it could be put right. And that's what I want to do
today.

Let me start with the past. After the Second World
War, Western Europe was rebuilt with the help of the
Marshall Plan, but it was still threatened by the Soviet
Union, which occupied the eastern part of the continent.
A group of visionaries led by Jean Monnet wanted to bind
the western part together into an organization whose
members would never wage war with one another. The
visionaries engaged in what Karl Popper called piecemeal
social engineering. They set limited but attainable goals,
established a time line, and generated public support,
knowing full well that each step would necessitate a further step forward. The European elite of our generation

responded enthusiastically. I personally regarded the European Union as the embodiment of an open society.

All went well until the Maastricht Treaty, which was signed in 1992. The architects knew that the treaty was incomplete: it created a central bank but did not establish a common treasury. They had reason to believe, however, that when the need arose, the necessary political will could be summoned and the next step forward would be taken.

Unfortunately, that is not what happened. Two things intervened: the collapse of the Soviet empire and the reunification of Germany, which were so intimately interrelated that they count as one event, and then came the crash of 2008, which is the second event.

Let me discuss German reunification first. Chancellor Helmut Kohl recognized that Germany could be reunited only in the context of a more united Europe. Under his farsighted leadership, Germany became the main driver of European integration. Germany was always willing to contribute a little bit extra so that every bargain could be turned into a win-win situation. President François Mitterrand wanted to tie Germany more closely into Europe without giving up too much national sovereignty. This Franco-German bargain was the foundation of the Maastricht Treaty.

Then came the Lisbon Treaty, which sought to transfer sovereignty to centralized institutions, notably the European Parliament and the Commission, but it was defeated by referenda in France and the Netherlands in 2005.

During the euro crisis that followed the crash of 2008, de facto political power migrated to the European Council, where the heads of state were able to make urgently needed decisions in the nick of time. This discrepancy between formal and de facto power is at the heart of what I call "The Tragedy of the European Union."

The crash of 2008 originated in the United States but hit the European banking system much harder. After 2008, a reunited Germany felt neither politically motivated nor rich enough to remain the motor of further integration.

Following the collapse of Lehman Brothers, the finance ministers of Europe declared that no other systemically important financial institutions would be allowed to fail, But Chancellor Angela Merkel insisted that every country should be responsible for its own banks. In doing so, she was reading German public opinion correctly. And that was the tipping point from integration to disintegration.

––––––

The European Union is now in an existential crisis. Most Europeans of my generation were supporters of further integration. Subsequent generations came to regard the EU as an enemy that deprives them of a secure and promising future. Many of them came to doubt whether the European Union can deal with a multiplicity of accumulated problems. This feeling was reinforced by the rise of anti-European, xenophobic parties that are motivated by values that are diametrically opposed to the values on which the European Union was founded.

Externally, the EU is surrounded by hostile powers—Putin's Russia, Erdogan's Turkey, Sisi's Egypt, and the America that Trump would like to create but can't.

Internally, the European Union has been governed by outdated treaties ever since the financial crisis of 2008. These treaties have become less and less relevant to prevailing conditions. Even the simplest innovations necessary to make the single currency sustainable could be introduced only by intergovernmental arrangements outside the existing treaties. That is how the functioning of European institutions became increasingly complicated and eventually rendered the EU itself dysfunctional in some ways.

The eurozone in particular became the exact opposite of what was originally intended. The European Union was meant to be a voluntary association of like-minded states that were willing to surrender part of their sovereignty for the common good. After the financial crisis of 2008, the eurozone was transformed into a creditor/debtor relationship, where the debtor countries couldn't meet their obligations and the creditor countries dictated the terms that they had to meet. By imposing an austerity policy, the creditor countries made it practically impossible for the debtors to grow out of their debts. The net result was neither voluntary nor equal.

———

If the European Union carries on with business as usual, there is little hope for an improvement. That is why the European Union needs to be radically reinvented. The top-down initiative started by Jean Monnet had carried the process of integration a long way, but it has lost its momentum. Now we need a collaborative effort that combines the top-down approach of the European institutions with the bottom-up initiatives that are necessary to engage the electorate.

Brexit will be an immensely damaging process, harmful to both sides. Most of the damage is felt right now, when the European Union is in an existential crisis, but its attention is diverted to negotiating the separation from Britain.

The European Union must resist the temptation to punish Britain and approach the negotiations in a constructive spirit. It should use Brexit as a catalyst for introducing far-reaching reforms. The divorce will be a drawn-out process taking as long as five years. Five years seems like an eternity in politics, especially in revolutionary times like the present. During that time, the European Union could transform itself into an organization that other countries like Britain would want to join. If that happened, the two sides may want to be reunited even before the divorce is completed. That would be a wonderful outcome, worth striving for. This seems practically inconceivable right now, but in reality, it is quite attainable. Britain is a parliamentary democracy. Within five years, it has to hold another general election, and the next parliament may vote to be reunited with Europe.

Such a Europe would differ from the current arrangements in two key respects. First, it would clearly distinguish between the European Union and the Eurozone. Second, it would recognize that the euro has many unsolved problems and they must not be allowed to destroy the European Union.

The eurozone is governed by outdated treaties that assert that all member states are expected to join the euro if and when they qualify. This has created an absurd situation where countries like Sweden, Poland, and the Czech Republic have made it clear that they have no intention of joining the euro, yet they are still described and treated as "pre-ins."

———

The effect is not purely cosmetic. It has converted the EU into an organization in which the eurozone constitutes the inner core, and the other members are relegated to an inferior position. There is a hidden assumption at work here, namely that various member states may be moving at various speeds, but they are all heading to the same destination. This has given rise to the claim of "an ever-closer union" that has been explicitly rejected by a number of countries.

This claim needs to be abandoned. Instead of a "multi-speed" Europe, we should aim for a "multitrack" Europe that would allow member states a wider variety of choices. This would have a far-reaching beneficial effect.

Right now, attitudes toward cooperation are negative: member states want to reassert their sovereignty rather than surrendering more of it. But if cooperation produced positive results, attitudes may improve and some objectives that are currently best pursued by coalitions of the willing may qualify for universal participation. There are three problem areas where meaningful progress is indispensable. The first is the refugee crisis; the second, territorial disintegration as exemplified by Brexit; the third, the lack of an economic growth policy.

We need to be realistic. In all three areas, we start from a very low base, and in the case of the refugee crisis, the trend is still downward. We still don't have a European migration policy. Each country pursues what it perceives to be its national interest, and it often works against the interests of other member states. Chancellor Merkel was right: the refugee crisis has the potential to destroy the European Union. But we mustn't give up. If we could make meaningful progress on alleviating the refugee crisis, the momentum would change in a positive direction.

I am a great believer in momentum. I call it reflexivity in my conceptual framework. And I can see a momentum developing that would change the European Union for the better. This would require a combination of top-down and bottom-up elements, and I can see both of them evolving.

Regarding the top-down political process, I kept my fingers crossed during the Dutch elections, in which the nationalist candidate Geert Wilders fell from first to second place. But I was greatly reassured by the outcome of the French elections, in which the only pro-European candidate among many achieved the seemingly impossible and emerged as the president of France. I am much more confident about the outcome of the German elections, where there are many combinations that could lead to a pro-European coalition, especially if the anti-European and xenophobic AfD continues its virtual collapse. The growing momentum may then be strong enough to overcome the biggest threat, the danger of a banking and migration crisis in Italy.

I can also see many spontaneous bottom-up initiatives, and significantly, they are mainly supported by young people. I have in mind the Pulse of Europe initiative, which started in Frankfurt in November and spread to some 120 cities across the continent; the Best for Britain movement in the United Kingdom; and the resistance to the PiS Party in Poland and to Fidesz in Hungary.

The resistance that Prime Minister Viktor Orbán encountered in Hungary must have surprised him as much as it surprised me. He sought to frame his policies as a personal conflict between the two of us and has made me the target of his unrelenting propaganda campaign. He cast himself in the role of the defender of Hungarian sovereignty and me as a shady currency speculator who uses his money to flood Europe—particularly his native Hungary—with illegal immigrants as part of some vague but nefarious plot.

This is the opposite of who I am. I am the proud founder of the Central European University that has, after twenty-six years, come to rank among the fifty best universities in the world in many of the social sciences. I have generously endowed the university, and that has enabled it to defend its academic freedom not only from interference by the Hungarian government but also from its founder.

I have strenuously resisted Orbán's attempts to translate our ideological differences into personal animosity and I have succeeded.

———————

What lessons have I learned from this experience? First, that to defend open societies, it is not enough to rely on the rule of law; you must also stand up for what you believe in. The university I have founded and the organizations that my foundation has supported are doing so. Their fate is in the balance. But I am confident that their determined defense of freedom—both academic freedom and the freedom of association—will eventually bring the slow-moving wheels of justice into motion. Second, I have learned that democracy cannot be imposed from the outside; it needs to be asserted and defended by the people themselves. I am full of admiration for the courageous way the Hungarian people have resisted the deception and corruption of the mafia state the Orbán regime has established. I'm also encouraged by the energetic way the European institutions have responded to the challenge emanating from Poland and Hungary. I find the proposal made by Germany to use the Cohesion Funds for enforcement purposes very promising. I can see the revival of the European Union gaining more and more ground. But it won't happen by itself. Those who care about the fate of Europe will have to get actively involved.

I must end with a word of caution. The European Union is cumbersome, slow moving, and often needs unanimity to enforce its rules. This is difficult to achieve when two countries, Poland and Hungary, are conspiring to oppose it. But the EU needs new rules to maintain its values. It can be done. But it will require resolute action by the European institutions and the active engagement of civil society. Let's get started!

The Refugee Crisis

(Excerpts from remarks delivered at the European Council on Foreign Relations on May 29, 2018.)

Since the financial crisis of 2008, the European Union seems to have lost its way. It adopted a program of fiscal retrenchment that led to the euro crisis. As a result, many young people today regard the European Union as an enemy that has deprived them of jobs and a secure and promising future. Populist politicians exploited the resentments and formed anti-European parties and movements.

Then came the refugee crisis of 2015. At first, most people sympathized with the plight of refugees fleeing from political repression or civil war, but they didn't want their everyday lives disrupted by a breakdown of social services. They were also disappointed by the failure of the authorities to cope with the crisis.

When that happened in Germany, the AfD was empowered, and it has grown into the largest opposition party. Italy has suffered from a similar experience recently, and the political repercussions have been even more disastrous: the anti-European parties almost took over the government. Italy is now facing elections in the midst of political chaos.

Indeed, the whole of Europe has been disrupted by the refugee crisis. Unscrupulous leaders have exploited it even in countries that have accepted hardly any refugees. In Hungary, Viktor Orbán based his reelection campaign on falsely accusing me of planning to flood Europe—Hungary included—with Muslim refugees.

He is now posing as the defender of his version of a Christian Europe that is challenging the values on which the European Union was founded. He is trying to take over the leadership of the Christian Democratic parties, which form the majority in the European Parliament.

In recent weeks not just Europe but the whole world has been shocked by President Trump's actions. He has unilaterally withdrawn from a nuclear arms treaty with Iran, thereby effectively destroying the transatlantic alliance. This development will put additional pressure of unpredictable force on an already beleaguered Europe. It is no longer a figure of speech to say that Europe is in existential danger; it is the harsh reality.

What can be done to save Europe?

Europe faces three pressing problems: the refugee crisis, territorial disintegrations as exemplified by Brexit, and the austerity policy that has hindered Europe's economic development. Bringing the refugee crisis under control may be the best place to start.

I have always advocated that the allocation of refugees within Europe should be entirely voluntary. Member states should not be forced to accept refugees they don't want, and refugees should not be forced to settle in countries where they don't want to go.

The voluntary principle ought to guide Europe's migration policy. Europe must also urgently reform or repeal the so-called Dublin Regulation, which has put an unfair burden on Italy and other Mediterranean countries, with disastrous political consequences.

The EU must protect its external borders but keep them open for lawful migrants. Member states, in turn, must not close their internal borders. The idea of a "fortress Europe" closed to political refugees and economic migrants alike violates both European and international law and, in any case, is totally unrealistic.

Europe wants to extend a helping hand toward Africa (and other parts of the developing world) by offering substantial assistance to democratically inclined regimes. This would enable them to provide education and employment to their citizens. They would be less likely to leave, and those who did would not qualify as refugees. At the same time, European countries could welcome migrants from these and other countries to meet their economic needs through an orderly process. In this way, migration would be voluntary on the part of both the migrants and the receiving states. Such a "Marshall Plan" would also help to reduce the number of political refugees by strengthening democratic regimes in the developing world.

Present-day reality falls substantially short of this ideal. First and most importantly, the European Union still doesn't have a unified migration policy. Each member state has its own policy, which is often at odds with the interests of other states.

Second, the main objective of most European countries is not to foster democratic development but to stem the flow of migrants. This diverts a large part of the available funds to dirty deals with dictators, bribing them to prevent migrants from passing through their territory or to use repressive measures to prevent their citizens from leaving. In the long run this will generate more political refugees.

Third, there is a woeful shortage of financial resources. We estimate that a meaningful Marshall Plan for Africa would require at least thirty billion euros a year for a number of years. Member states could contribute only a small fraction of this amount, even if they were ready to do so.

How might such a plan be financed, then? It's important to recognize that the refugee crisis is a European problem and needs a European solution. The European Union has a high credit rating, and its borrowing capacity is largely unused. When should that capacity be put to use if not in an existential crisis? Throughout history, the national debt always grew during times of war. Admittedly, adding to the national debt runs counter to the prevailing addiction to austerity, but the austerity policy is itself a contributing factor to the crisis in which Europe finds itself.

"Europe, Please Wake Up"

(Article published on *Project Syndicate* on February 11, 2019.)

Europe is sleepwalking into oblivion, and the people of Europe need to wake up before it is too late. If they don't, the European Union will go the way of the Soviet Union in 1991. Neither our leaders nor ordinary citizens seem to understand that we are experiencing a revolutionary moment, that the range of possibilities is very broad, and that the eventual outcome is thus highly uncertain.

Most of us assume that the future will more or less resemble the present, but this is not necessarily so. In a long and eventful life, I have witnessed many periods of what I call radical disequilibrium. We are living in such a period today.

The next inflection point will be the elections for the European Parliament in May 2019. Unfortunately, anti-European forces will enjoy a competitive advantage in the balloting. There are several reasons for this, including the outdated party system that prevails in most European countries, the practical impossibility of treaty change, and the lack of legal tools for disciplining member states that violate the principles on which the European Union was founded. The EU can impose the *acquis communautaire* (the body of European Union law) on applicant countries but lacks sufficient capacity to enforce member states' compliance.

The antiquated party system hampers those who want to preserve the values on which the EU was founded, but it helps those who want to replace those values with something radically different. This is true in individual countries and even more so in trans-European alliances.

The party system of individual states reflects the divisions that mattered in the nineteenth and twentieth centuries, such as the conflict between capital and labor. But the cleavage that matters most today is between pro- and anti-European forces.

The EU's dominant country is Germany, and the dominant political alliance in Germany—between the Christian Democratic Union (CDU) and the Bavaria-based Christian Social Union (CSU)—has become unsustainable. The alliance worked as long as there was no significant party in Bavaria to the right of the CSU. That changed with the rise of the extremist Alternative für Deutschland (AfD). In last September's länder elections, the CSU's result was its worst in over six decades, and the AfD entered the Bavarian Parliament for the first time.

The AfD's rise removed the raison d'être of the CDU-CSU alliance. But that alliance cannot be broken up without triggering new elections that neither Germany nor Europe can afford. As it is, the current ruling coalition cannot be as robustly pro-European as it would be without the AfD threatening its right flank.

The situation is far from hopeless. The German Greens have emerged as the only consistently pro-European party in the country, and they continue rising in opinion polls, whereas the AfD seems to have reached its high point (except in the former East Germany). But now CDU-CSU voters are represented by a party whose commitment to European values is ambivalent.

In the United Kingdom, too, an antiquated party structure prevents the popular will from finding proper expression. Both Labour and the Conservatives are internally divided, but their leaders—Jeremy Corbyn and Theresa May, respectively—are so determined to deliver Brexit that they have agreed to cooperate to attain it. The situation is so complicated that most Britons just want to get it over with, although it will be the defining event for the country for decades to come.

But the collusion between Corbyn and May has aroused opposition in both parties, which, in the case of Labour, is bordering on rebellion. The day after Corbyn and May met, May announced a program to aid impoverished pro-Brexit Labour constituencies in the north of England. Corbyn is now accused of betraying the pledge he made at Labour's September 2018 party conference to back a second Brexit referendum if holding an election is not possible.

The public is also becoming aware of the dire consequences of Brexit. The chances that May's deal will be rejected on February 14 are growing by the day. That could set in motion a groundswell of support for a referendum or, even better, revoking Britain's Article 50 notification.

Italy finds itself in a similar predicament. The EU made a fatal mistake in 2017 by strictly enforcing the Dublin

Regulation, which unfairly burdens countries like Italy, where migrants first enter the EU. This drove Italy's predominantly pro-European and pro-immigration electorate into the arms of the anti-European League Party and the Five Star Movement in 2018. The previously dominant Democratic Party is in disarray. As a result, the significant portion of the electorate that remains pro-European has no party to vote for. There is, however, an attempt underway to organize a united pro-European list. A similar reordering of party systems is happening in France, Poland, Sweden, and probably elsewhere.

When it comes to trans-European alliances, the situation is even worse. National parties at least have some roots in the past, but the trans-European alliances are entirely dictated by party leaders' self-interest. The European People's Party (EPP) is the worst offender. The EPP is almost entirely devoid of principles, as demonstrated by its willingness to permit the continued membership of Hungarian prime minister Viktor Orbán's Fidesz in order to preserve its majority and control the allocation of top jobs in the EU. Anti-European forces may look good in comparison: at least they have some principles, even if they are odious.

It is difficult to see how the pro-European parties can emerge victorious from the election in May unless they put Europe's interests ahead of their own. One can still make a case for preserving the EU in order to radically reinvent it. But that would require a change of heart in the EU. The current leadership is reminiscent of the politburo when the Soviet Union collapsed—continuing to issue *ukazes* as if they were still relevant.

The first step to defending Europe from its enemies, both internal and external, is to recognize the magnitude of the threat they present. The second is to awaken the sleeping pro-European majority and mobilize it to defend the values on which the EU was founded. Otherwise, the dream of a united Europe could become the nightmare of the twenty-first century.

Europe's Silent Majority Speaks Out
(Article published on *Project Syndicate* on June 7, 2019.)

Last month's elections to the European Parliament produced better results than one could have expected, and for a simple reason: the silent pro-European majority has spoken. What they said is that they want to preserve the values on which the European Union was founded, but that they also want radical changes in the way the EU functions. Their main concern is climate change.

This favors the pro-European parties, especially the Greens. The anti-European parties, which cannot be expected to do anything constructive, failed to make the gains that they expected. Nor can they form the united front that they would need in order to become more influential.

One of the institutions that needs to be changed is the Spitzenkandidat system. It is supposed to provide a form of indirect selection of the EU leadership. In fact, as Franklin Dehousse has explained in a brilliant but pessimistic article in the *EU Observer*, it is worse than no democratic selection at all. Each member state has real political parties, but their trans-European combination produces artificial constructs that serve no purpose other than to promote the personal ambitions of their leaders.

This can best be seen in the European People's Party (EPP), which has managed to capture the presidency of the Commission since 2004. The EPP's current leader, Manfred Weber, who has no experience in a national government, appears willing to enter into practically any compromise in order to remain in the parliamentary majority. That includes embracing Hungary's autocratic prime minister, Viktor Orbán.

Orbán has posed a serious problem for Weber, because Orbán has openly flouted European norms and established what amounts to a mafia state. Nearly half the national parties constituting the EPP wanted to expel Orbán's party, Fidesz. Instead of following through, however, Weber managed to convince the EPP to make a relatively easy demand on Fidesz: allow the Central European University (CEU, which I founded) to continue functioning freely in Hungary as an American university.

Fidesz failed to comply. Even so, the EPP did not expel Fidesz, but merely suspended it so that it could be counted as part of the EPP when the president of the Commission is chosen. Orbán is now trying to reestablish Fidesz as a bona fide member of the EPP. It will be interesting to see if Weber finds a way to accommodate him.

The Spitzenkandidat system is not based on an intergovernmental agreement, so it could easily be changed. It would be much better if the president of the European Commission were directly elected from a carefully selected list of qualified candidates, but that would require treaty changes. The President of the European Council could continue to be elected by a qualified majority of the member states, as the Treaty of Lisbon prescribes.

The reform that would require treaty changes is justified by the increased democratic legitimacy conferred by the European Parliamentary elections. Turnout in the recent election surpassed 50 percent, up sharply from 42.6 percent in 2014. This is the first time that turnout has increased at all since the first election in 1979, when 62 percent of eligible voters participated.

Strangely enough, on this occasion, the Spitzenkandidat system promises to produce a dream team. French President Emmanuel Macron, who is opposed to the Spitzenkandidat system as a matter of principle, is largely responsible for this development. At a dinner with Spanish Prime Minister Pedro Sánchez, the winner of Spain's national general election, which preceded the European Parliament vote, the two leaders agreed to support two Spitzenkandidaten who would be ideal for the Commission and for the Council.

Germany is the main supporter of the Spitzenkandidat system. If Weber loses out, Germany will be pushing for Jens Weidmann, President of the Bundesbank, to become President of the ECB. He would hardly be ideal. In fact, he is disqualified by the fact that he testified before Germany's Federal Constitutional Court against the ECB in a case seeking to invalidate the Bank's so-called outright monetary transactions, a policy that was crucial to overcoming the eurozone crisis earlier this decade. I hope this fact will become more widely known.

Any other qualified candidate would be preferable to Weidmann as ECB president. As things stand now, France will not have any of the top jobs. It would be a good thing if Germany didn't have one either, because it would leave more room for other countries.

There are many EU institutions aside from the Spitzenkandidat system that require radical reform. But that can wait until we find out whether, and to what extent, the promise held out by the parliamentary election results is realized. This is not yet the time to declare victory, relax, and celebrate. There is a lot of work to be done to turn the EU into a well-functioning organization that fulfills its great potential.

Post-Script
(August 5, 2019)

It is truly amazing that a dysfunctional system of choosing leaders has managed to produce the strongest leadership the European Union has enjoyed since the days of Jacques Delors. How did this happen?

The *spitzenkandidat* system was abandoned because Manfred Weber was widely rejected as totally unqualified. President Macron and Chancellor Merkel then came up with an inspired choice, Ursula von der Leyen. She is a more committed pro-European than anybody else in the CDU leadership with the possible exception of Norbert Röttgen, the chairman of the Committee on Foreign Affairs in the Bundestag. But the appointment came as a total surprise to everyone, von der Leyen included, and it aroused considerable opposition in the European Parliament among those who were committed to the spitzenkandidat system. This made the parliamentary confirmation process very difficult. She barely squeezed through with a razor-thin majority. She made a number of commitments that will increase the influence of the European Parliament over the European Commission. This may weaken her hand.

The situation has had a harmful side-effect: Viktor Orbán claims to be responsible for von der Leyen's election. I am convinced that his claim is false, but there is no way to prove it because the vote was secret. As a consequence Orbán's claim is widely accepted and provides fodder to

IN DEFENSE OF OPEN SOCIETY

those who remain opposed to her. After the recent meeting between von der Leyen and Orbán, Orbán applauded their closeness, but von der Leyen emphasized that the Fidesz government's respect for the rule of law was the main subject of discussion—a substantial difference.

Orbán is playing a duplicitous game. On the one hand he wants to remain a member of the European People's Party; on the other, he continues to commit egregious violations of European law. He has abolished the independence of the Hungarian Academy of Science and taken away the properties belonging to it. The membership is up in arms but it is not getting the support of the EU that it deserves. I hope this will be high on the President's agenda.

Having lost out with Manfred Weber, Germany started pushing Jens Weidmann for President of the European Central Bank. Fortunately, the job went to a much better candidate, Christine Lagarde. This created a vacancy at the International Monetary Fund (IMF), which will be filled by Kristalina Georgieva of the World Bank. This will have the additional benefit that the IMF and the World Bank, where Georgieva remains influential, will work more closely together than in any time in their history. Gender- and regional balance has also been achieved. Things could not have worked out better.

I am an enthusiastic supporter of President Macron's proposal that Guy Verhofstadt should be appointed to form a working group to explore better alternatives to the spitzencandidat system. Their report will take more than a year to prepare and is bound to be very controversial when it is published. This will allow both the European Commission and Parliament to make some progress on issues, such as climate change, on which there is greater consensus. In any case, the newly elected leaders of the EU will have their work cut out for them to fulfill the high expectations attached to their appointment.

CHAPTER 6

My Conceptual Framework

"My Understanding of Reflexivity Enabled Me Both to Anticipate the Financial Crisis and to Deal with It When It Struck"

(This is a condensed version of an article published in the *Journal of Economic Methodology* on January 13, 2014.)

SECTION 1:
INTRODUCTION

Reflexivity, the idea central to my conceptual framework, was not discovered by me. Earlier observers recognized it—or, at least, aspects of it—often under a different name. Frank Knight (1921) explored the difference between risk and uncertainty. John Maynard Keynes (1936, chap. 12) compared financial markets to a beauty contest, where the participants had to guess who would be the most popular choice. The sociologist Robert Merton (1949) wrote about self-fulfilling prophecies, unintended consequences, and the bandwagon effect. Karl Popper spoke of the "Oedipus effect" in the *Poverty of Historicism* (1957, chap. 5).

My own conceptual framework has its origins in my time as a student at the London School of Economics in the late 1950s. I took my final exams one year early, so I had a year to fill before I was qualified to receive my degree. I could choose my tutor, and I chose Popper, whose book *The Open Society and Its Enemies* (1945) had made a profound impression on me.

In Popper's other great work, *The Logic of Scientific Discovery* (1935/1959), he argued that the empirical truth cannot be known with absolute certainty. Even scientific laws cannot be verified beyond a shadow of a doubt: they can only be falsified by testing. One failed test is enough to falsify, but no amount of conforming instances is sufficient to verify. Scientific laws are always hypothetical in character, and their validity remains open to falsification.

While I was reading Popper, I was also studying economic theory, and I was struck by the contradiction between Popper's emphasis on imperfect understanding and the theory of perfect competition in economics, which postulated perfect knowledge. This led me to start questioning the assumptions of economic theory. I replaced the postulates of rational expectations and efficient markets with my own principles of fallibility and reflexivity.

After college, I started working in the financial markets, where I had not much use for the economic theories I had studied in college. Strangely enough, the conceptual framework I had developed under Popper's influence provided me with much more valuable insights. And while I was engaged in making money, I did not lose my interest in philosophy.

I published my first book, *The Alchemy of Finance*, in 1987. In that book, I tried to explain the philosophical underpinnings of my approach to financial markets. The book attracted a certain amount of attention. It has been read by most people in the hedge fund industry, and it is taught in business schools. But the philosophical arguments in that book and subsequent books (Soros 1998, 2000) did not make much of an impression on the economics departments of universities. My framework was largely dismissed as the conceit of a man who has been successful in business and, therefore, fancies himself as a philosopher. With my theories largely ignored by academia, I began to regard myself as a failed philosopher—I even gave a lecture at the University of Vienna in 1995 entitled "A Failed

Philosopher Tries Again." Inspired by the height of the cathedral, I decreed the "doctrine of fallibility."

All that changed as a result of the financial crash of 2008. My understanding of reflexivity enabled me both to anticipate the crisis and to deal with it when it finally struck (Soros 2008, 2009). When the fallout of the crisis spread from the United States to Europe and around the world, it enabled me to explain and predict events better than most others (Soros 2012). The crisis put in stark relief the failings of orthodox economic theory (Soros 2010). As people realized how badly traditional economics has failed, interest in reflexivity grew.

In this essay, I will articulate my current thinking. In Section 2, I will explain the concepts of fallibility and reflexivity in general terms. In Section 3, I will discuss the implications of my conceptual framework for the social sciences in general and for economics in particular. In Section 4, I will describe how my conceptual framework applies to the financial markets, with special attention to financial bubbles and the ongoing euro crisis. I will then conclude with some thoughts on the need for a new paradigm in social science.

SECTION 2: FALLIBILITY, REFLEXIVITY, AND THE HUMAN UNCERTAINTY PRINCIPLE

My conceptual framework is built on two relatively simple propositions. The first I call the *principle of fallibility*. In situations that have thinking participants, their views of the world never perfectly correspond to the actual state of affairs. People can gain knowledge of individual facts, but when it comes to formulating theories or forming an overall view, their perspective is bound to be either biased or inconsistent or both.

The second proposition is what I call the *principle of reflexivity*. The imperfect views that people hold can influence or change the state of affairs through their actions. For example, if investors believe that markets are efficient, then that belief will change the way they invest, which in turn will change the behavior of the markets in which they are participating.

The two principles are tied together like Siamese twins, but fallibility is the firstborn: without fallibility, there could be no reflexivity. Both principles can be observed operating in the real world. So when my critics say that I am merely stating the obvious, they are right— but only up to a point. What makes my propositions interesting is that they contradict some of the basic tenets of economic theory. My conceptual framework deserves attention not because it constitutes a new discovery but because something as commonsensical as reflexivity has been so studiously ignored by economists. The field of economics has gone to great lengths to eliminate the uncertainty associated with reflexivity in order to formulate universally valid laws similar to Newtonian physics. In doing so, economists set themselves an impossible task. The uncertainty associated with fallibility and reflexivity is inherent in the human condition. To make this point, I lump together the two concepts as the *human uncertainty principle.*

Fallibility

The complexity of the world in which we live exceeds our capacity to comprehend it. Confronted by a reality of extreme complexity, we are obliged to resort to various methods of simplification: generalizations, dichotomies, metaphors, decision rules, and moral precepts, just to mention a few.

The structure of the brain is another source of fallibility. Recent advances in brain science have begun to provide some insight into how the brain functions, and they have substantiated David Hume's insight that reason is the slave of passion. The idea of a disembodied intellect or reason is a figment of our imagination.

Reflexivity

The concept of reflexivity applies exclusively to situations that have thinking participants. The participants' thinking serves two functions. One is to understand the world in which we live; I call this the *cognitive function.* The other is to make an impact on the world and to advance the participants' interests; I call this the *manipulative function*. I use the term "manipulative" to emphasize intentionality.

The two functions connect the participants' thinking—which I refer to as *subjective reality*—and the actual state of affairs—which can be described as *objective reality*—in opposite directions. In the cognitive function, the participant is cast in the role of a passive observer: the direction of causation is from the world to the mind. In the manipulative function, the participants play an active role: the direction of causation is from the mind to the world. Both functions are subject to fallibility. When both functions are at work at the same time, they affect both subjective and objective reality. Because of fallibility, the outcome rarely corresponds to the agents' intentions.

Lack of an Independent Criterion of Truth

If the cognitive function operated in isolation, without any interference from the manipulative function, it could produce knowledge. Knowledge is represented by true statements. A statement is true if it corresponds to the facts. But if the manipulative function is at work, the facts no longer serve as an independent criterion of truth.

Consider the statement "It is raining." That statement is true or false depending on whether it is, in fact, raining. Whether people believe it is raining or not cannot change the facts. The agent can assess the statement without any interference from the manipulative function and, thus, gain knowledge.

Now consider the statement "I love you." The statement is reflexive. It will have an effect on the object of affection, and the recipient's response may then affect the feelings of the person making the statement, changing the truth value of the statement. Since the response comes later than the original statement, reflexivity often leads to feedback loops.

The feedback loop connects the realms of beliefs and events. Since both the cognitive and manipulative functions are subject to fallibility, the uncertainty associated with reflexivity is introduced into both realms. The process may be initiated from either direction, from a change in views or from a change in circumstances.

There is only one objective reality, but there are as many different subjective views as there are thinking participants. The views can be divided into different groups—such as doubters and believers, trend followers and contrarians, Cartesians and empiricists—but these are simplifications, and the categories are not fixed. Agents may hold views that are not easily categorized; moreover, they are free to choose between categories and are free to switch.

In extreme cases, the process may occur within a solitary individual—for example, a person asking herself who she is and what she stands for, which leads her to take actions, which in turn affect her perceptions of her identity. This might be called self-reflexivity.

Reflexive Systems

Let me illustrate the complex relationship between thinking and reality with the help of a diagram. Figure 1 describes the roles of the cognitive and manipulative functions, fallibility, reflexivity, and intentionality. Together this might be thought of as a reflexive system.

I have indicated the presence of multiple participants and, therefore, multiple subjective realities. Nevertheless, the diagram is inadequate because it would require three dimensions to show the multiple participants interacting with each other as well as with the objective aspect of reality.

The Human Uncertainty Principle

The economist Frank Knight (1921) introduced an important distinction between risk and uncertainty. Risk is when there are multiple possible future states and the probabilities of those different future states occurring are known. Risk is well defined by the laws of probability and statistics. Knightian uncertainty occurs when the probabilities of future states or even the nature of possible future states is not known.

Fallibility is a key source of Knightian uncertainty in human affairs, but it is by no means the only one. For instance, different participants have different goals,

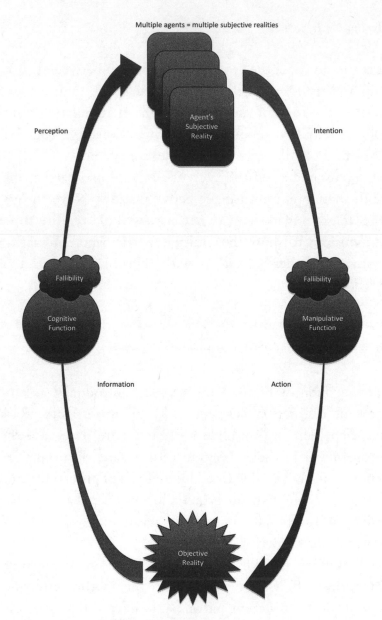

Multiple agents = multiple subjective realities

Agent's
Subjective
Reality

Perception

Intention

Fallibility

Fallibility

Cognitive
Function

Manipulative
Function

Information

Action

Objective
Reality

FIGURE 1. A reflexive system.

some of which may be in conflict with each other. Moreover, as Isaiah Berlin pointed out, each participant may be guided by a multiplicity of values that may not be self-consistent. The uncertainties created by these factors are more extensive than those specifically associated with reflexivity.

We must also remember that not all forms of fallibility create Knightian uncertainty. Some forms are subject to statistical analysis—human errors leading to road accidents, for example.

Humans face quantifiable risks as well as Knightian uncertainty. There are many activities that are predictable, or at least their probabilities can be calculated. Behavioral economists have catalogued many regularities in human behavior, but with few exceptions, these experiments do not deal with reflexivity. Most behavioral experiments assess people's perception of objective reality (e.g., trying to remember numbers, guess probabilities of different events, and so on) and, thus, are really measures of the fallibility of the cognitive function. The manipulative function is rarely studied.

Earlier, I referred to the combination of reflexivity and fallibility as the human uncertainty principle. That makes it a broader concept than reflexivity. It is much more specific and stringent than the subjective skepticism that pervades Cartesian philosophy. It gives us objective reasons why the theories held by participants are liable to be biased, incomplete, or both.

SECTION 3: PHILOSOPHY OF
SOCIAL SCIENCE

The idea that the sciences should be unified goes back to the pre-Socratic Greeks and has been a subject of debate in philosophy ever since. Popper (1935/1959, 1957) argued that science could be demarcated from metaphysics by his notion of falsifiable hypotheses and, moreover, that falsifiable hypotheses could also provide methodological unity to the sciences.

Although I have drawn much inspiration from Popper, this is an important point where I differ from my mentor. I believe that reflexivity provides a strong challenge to the idea that natural and social sciences can be unified. I believe that social science can still be a valuable human endeavor, but in order for it to be so, we must recognize its fundamental differences from natural science.

Popper's Theory of Scientific Method

I base my argument on Popper's (1935/1959) theory of scientific method. One of Popper's key insights was that scientific laws are hypothetical in character; they cannot be verified, but they can be falsified by empirical testing. The key to the success of scientific method is that it can test generalizations of universal validity with the help of singular observations. One failed test is sufficient to falsify a theory, but no amount of confirming instances is sufficient to verify it. Generalizations that cannot be tested do not qualify as scientific.

This is a brilliant construct that makes science both empirical and rational. According to Popper, it is empirical because we test our theories by observing whether the predictions we derive from them are true, and it is rational because we use deductive logic in doing so. Popper dispenses with inductive logic, which he considers invalid, and gives testing a central role instead. He also makes a strong case for critical thinking by asserting that scientific laws are only provisionally valid and remain open to reexamination. The three salient features of Popper's scheme are the symmetry between prediction and explanation, the asymmetry between verification and falsification, and the central role of testing. These three features allow science to grow, improve, and innovate.

Problems of Social Science

Popper's scheme has worked extraordinarily well for the study of natural phenomena, but the human uncertainty principle throws a monkey wrench into the supreme simplicity and elegance of Popper's scheme. The symmetry between prediction and explanation is destroyed because the future is genuinely uncertain and, therefore, cannot be predicted with the same degree of certainty as it can be explained in retrospect. One might object that uncertainty exists in all realms of science. But while Werner

Heisenberg's Uncertainty Principle in quantum mechanics is subject to the laws of probability and statistics, the deep Knightian uncertainties of human affairs associated with the human uncertainty principle are not.

Even more importantly, the central role of testing is endangered. Should the initial and final conditions include or exclude the participants' thinking? The question is important because testing requires replicating those conditions. If the participants' thinking is included, it is difficult to determine what the initial and final conditions are because the participants' views can only be inferred from their statements or actions. If the participants' thinking is excluded, the initial and final conditions do not constitute singular observations because the same objective conditions may be associated with very different subjective views. In either case, testing cannot meet the requirements of Popper's scheme. This limitation does not preclude social sciences from producing worthwhile generalizations, but they are unlikely to match the predictive power of the laws of physics. Empirical testing ought to play a central role in social science as well, but it should not be expected to produce universal and timeless generalizations. This point will be elaborated at the end of Section 4.

The Structure of Events

I contend that situations that have thinking participants have a different structure from natural phenomena. The

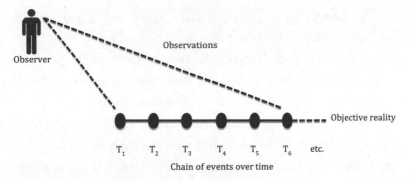

FIGURE 2. A chain of cause and effect.

difference lies in the role thinking plays. In natural phenomena, thinking plays no causal role. Events unfold irrespective of the views held by the observers. The structure of natural events can be described as a chain of cause and effect, generating a stream of objective facts, without any interference from the subjective aspects of reality (see Figure 2).

In natural science, the outside observer is engaged only in the cognitive function, and the facts provide a reliable criterion by which the truth of the observers' theories can be judged. So the outside observers can obtain knowledge about the natural phenomena they are observing. Based on that knowledge, nature can be successfully manipulated. That manipulation may change the state of the physical world, but it does not change the laws that govern that world. We can use our understanding of the physical world to create airplanes, but the invention of the airplane did not change the laws of aerodynamics.

By contrast, in human affairs, thinking is *part of* the subject matter. The course of events leads not only from facts to facts but also from facts to the participants' perceptions (the cognitive function) and from the participants' decisions to facts (the manipulative function).

Figure 3 is a simplified presentation of the structure of social events. It illustrates that there is only one objective aspect but as many subjective aspects of reality as there are thinking participants. The reflexive feedback loops between the objective and subjective aspects of reality create a lace-like pattern, which is superimposed on the direct line leading from one set of facts to the next and deflects it from what it would be if there were no feedback loops. The feedback sometimes brings the subjective and objective aspects closer together and sometimes drives them further apart. The two aspects are aligned, but only

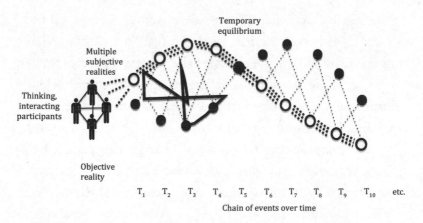

FIGURE 3. Social phenomena.

loosely—the human uncertainty principle implies that a perfect alignment is the exception rather than the rule.

Physics Envy

Popper's scheme would require social scientists to produce generalizations of universal and timeless validity that determine the alignment of the objective and subjective aspects of reality. If the human uncertainty principle is valid, that is an impossible task. Yet the achievements of natural science, exemplified by Newtonian physics, were so alluring that economists and other social scientists have tried incredibly hard to establish such generalizations. They suffered from what I like to call "physics envy." In order to achieve the impossible, they invented or postulated some kind of fixed relationship between the participants' thinking and the actual course of events. Karl Marx asserted that the material conditions of production determined the ideological superstructure; Freud maintained that people's behavior was determined by the unconscious. Both claimed scientific status for their theories, but Popper rightly argued that their theories could not be falsified by testing.

However, Popper did not go far enough. The same argument applies to the mainstream economic theory currently taught in universities. It is an axiomatic system based on deductive logic, not on empirical evidence (the most popular book used to teach graduate students microeconomics is over one thousand pages long, with numerous axiomatic proofs in it, but not a single fact). If the axioms are true, so are the mathematical deductions. In this regard, economic theory resembles Euclidian geometry. But Euclid's postulates are modeled on conditions prevailing in the real world, while at least some of the postulates of economics, notably rational choice and rational expectations, are dictated by the desire to imitate Newtonian physics rather than real-world evidence.

This ill-fated attempt by economists to slavishly imitate physics has a long history. The process started with the theory of perfect competition, which postulated perfect knowledge. That postulate was later modified to universally available perfect information. When that postulate proved inadequate, Lionel Robbins, who was my professor at the London School of Economics, defined the task of economics as the allocation of limited means to unlimited alternative ends (Robbins 1932). He specifically excluded the study of the means and the ends themselves. By taking the prevailing values and methods of production as given, he eliminated reflexivity as a possible subject of study for economics. Subsequently, this approach reached its apex with the rational expectations and efficient market hypotheses in the 1960s and 1970s.

To be sure, physics envy is not unjustified. The achievements of natural science stand as convincing testimony to man's ability to use reason. Unfortunately, these achievements do not ensure that human behavior is always governed by reason.

Human Uncertainty as an Impediment
to Scientific Method

The human uncertainty principle not only prevents the social sciences from producing results comparable to physics; it interferes with scientific method in other ways as well. I shall mention only one of them.

As we have seen, natural phenomena provide a genuinely independent criterion for judging the validity of generalizations, but the facts produced by social processes do not do so because they are influenced by theories held by participants. This makes social theories themselves subject to reflexivity. In other words, they serve not only a cognitive but also a manipulative function.

To be sure, the generalizations and observations of natural scientists are also theory laden, and they influence the selection of facts but do not influence the facts themselves. Heisenberg's Uncertainty Principle showed that the act of observation impacts a quantum system. But the discovery of the uncertainty principle itself did not alter the behavior of quantum particles one iota. The principle applied before Heisenberg discovered it and will continue to apply long after human observers are gone. But social theories— whether Marxism, market fundamentalism, or the theory of reflexivity—can affect the subject matter to which they refer.

Scientific method is supposed to be devoted to the pursuit of truth. But why should social science confine itself to passively studying social phenomena when it can also actively change the state of affairs? The temptation to use social theories to change reality rather than to understand it is much greater than in natural science. Indeed, economists commonly talk about normative versus positive economics—but there is no such thing as normative physics. That is a fundamental difference between natural and social sciences that needs to be recognized.

A Spectrum Between Physical and Social Sciences

In my argument, I have drawn a sharp distinction between the social and natural sciences. But such dichotomies are usually not found in reality; rather, we introduce them in our efforts to make some sense out of an otherwise confusing reality. Indeed, while the dichotomy between physics and social sciences seems clear-cut, there are other sciences, such as biology and the study of animal societies, that occupy intermediate positions.

The distinction I have drawn between natural and social science consists of the presence or absence of thinking participants' who have a will of their own. That begs the question of what constitutes a "thinking participant." One might reasonably ask whether a chimpanzee, a dolphin, or a computerized stock-trading program is a thinking participant. In some fields, superior data-crunching capacity may trump the human imagination, as the chess contest between Big Blue and Gary Kasparov has shown. And automatic trading systems appear to be currently outperforming hedge funds run by humans. However, I would note that humans have some unique characteristics, notably language, emotions, and culture. Both our individual and shared subjective realities are far richer and more complex than any other creature's, including the products of artificial intelligence.

Clearly there are some problems that set natural and social science apart. I have focused on reflexivity. It presents itself in both the subject matter and its scientific study so that it may be treated as two closely interrelated problems. In the subject matter, the problem presents itself as the human uncertainty principle. That has no equivalent in natural science. For scientific method, the problem is more complicated because scientists are also human beings and their thinking also serves two functions. This problem presents itself in both natural and social science, but an analysis of the various possible solutions yields different results.

Science is a discipline that seeks to perfect the cognitive function by artificially isolating itself from the manipulative function. It does so by submitting itself to a number of conventions such as insisting on empirical tests that can be replicated and/or observed by others. Popper's scheme shows what natural science can achieve by obeying those rules and conventions. As I have shown, the human uncertainty principle prevents social science from matching these achievements. But there is also a flip side to be considered: What happens when those rules and conventions are not observed? Remember that my criterion of demarcation between natural and social science is that the latter is reflexive; the former is not. In other words, social science can change objective reality by influencing the participants' views, but natural science cannot do so because its subject matter has no thinking participants. That is what I meant when I remarked in *The Alchemy of Finance* that the alchemists made a mistake in trying to change the nature of base metals by incantation; instead, they should have focused their attention on the financial markets, where they could have succeeded. Now I need to take my analysis further.

Natural science can work wonders as long as it follows Popper's scheme because it has a purely objective criterion, namely the facts, by which the truth or validity of its laws can be judged, but it cannot produce anything worthwhile by cheating on the testing process. Cars that do not obey the laws of physics will not move; airplanes will not fly.

How about social science? We have seen that, according to Popper's scheme, it cannot be expected to produce results comparable to the natural sciences. Conversely, social theories also serve a manipulative function, and their influence on objective reality may be quite successful in achieving their goal—at least for a while, until objective reality reasserts itself and the outcome fails to correspond to expectations. There are many manipulative statements that fit this pattern. President Obama managed to make the post–2008 recession shorter and shallower by asserting that the economy was fundamentally sound and promising a speedy recovery, but he paid a heavy political price when reality failed to live up to his promises. Fed chairman Alan Greenspan was a masterful manipulator, and his Delphic utterances were more difficult to prove wrong. Both Freud and Marx sought to gain acceptance for their theories by claiming scientific status.

One of the most interesting cases is the efficient market hypothesis and its political companion, market fundamentalism. We shall see that the mechanism that provides some degree of justification for the claim that markets are always right is reflexivity, not rational expectations. Yet a false explanation can be subjectively more appealing than what I consider to be the true one. The efficient market hypothesis allows economic theory to lay claim to the status of a hard science like physics. And market fundamentalism allows the financially successful to claim that they are serving the public interest by pursuing their self-interest. That is a powerful combination that dominated the field until it caused a lot of damage in the financial crisis of 2007–2008. Surprisingly, it survived that debacle: the conservative wing of the Republican Party managed to pin the blame for the financial crisis on the government rather than on the private sector.

The Limits and Promise of Social Science

Interestingly, both Karl Popper and Friedrich Hayek recognized in their famous exchange in the pages of

Economica (Popper 1944) that the social sciences cannot produce results comparable with physics. Hayek inveighed against the mechanical and uncritical application of the quantitative methods of natural science. He called it "scientism," and Popper wrote *The Poverty of Historicism* (1957), in which he argued that history is not determined by universally valid scientific laws. Nevertheless, Popper proclaimed what he called the "doctrine of the unity of method," by which he meant that both natural and social sciences should use the same methods and be judged by the same criteria.

By proclaiming the doctrine, Popper sought to distinguish pseudo-scientific theories like those of Marx and Freud from mainstream economics. As mentioned earlier, Popper did not go far enough: rational choice theory and the efficient market hypothesis are just as pseudo-scientific as Marxist and Freudian theories.

As I see it, the implication of the human uncertainty principle is that the subject matter of the natural and social sciences is fundamentally different; therefore, they need to develop different methods and should be held to different standards. Economic theory should not be expected to meet the standards established by Newtonian physics. In fact, if it did produce universally valid laws, economic profit itself would be impossible, as Knight (1921, 28) pointed out:

> If all changes were to take place in accordance with invariable and universally known laws, [so that] they

could be foreseen for an indefinite period in advance
of their occurrence, . . . profit or loss would not arise.

I contend that Popper's scheme cannot produce results in the human sphere comparable with the amazing
achievements of physics. The slavish imitation of natural
science can easily produce misleading results, sometimes
with disastrous consequences. Look at the consequences
of rational expectations theory: it prevented economists
from recognizing reflexivity and encouraged the development of synthetic financial instruments and risk-manage-
ment techniques that ignore Knightian uncertainty.

My contention begs the question of what social scientists should do, what methods they should use, and by
what criteria they should be judged. I have only a par-
tial answer. Any valid methodology of social science must
explicitly recognize both fallibility and reflexivity and
the Knightian uncertainty they create. Empirical testing
ought to remain a decisive criterion for judging whether
a theory qualifies as scientific, but in light of the human
uncertainty principle in social systems, it cannot always
be as rigorous as Popper's scheme requires. Nor can universally and timelessly valid theories be expected to yield
determinate predictions because future events are contingent on future decisions, which are bound to be fallible.
In economics, contingent, time- and context-bound theories may yield more useful explanations and predictions
than timeless and universal generalizations based on un-
grounded assumptions.

SECTION 4:
FINANCIAL MARKETS

Financial markets provide an excellent laboratory for testing the ideas I have put forward in the previous sections. The course of events is easier to observe than in most other areas. Many of the facts take a quantitative form, and the data are well recorded and well preserved. The opportunity for testing occurs because my interpretation of financial markets directly contradicts the efficient market hypothesis, which has been the prevailing paradigm.

The efficient market hypothesis claims that markets tend toward equilibrium and that deviations occur in a random fashion and can be attributed to exogenous shocks. It is then a testable proposition whether the efficient market hypothesis or my theory of reflexivity is better at explaining and predicting events. I contend that my theory of reflexivity is superior, even in its current rudimentary stage of development, for explaining and predicting financial markets in general and historical events like the financial crisis of 2007–2008 and the subsequent euro crisis in particular.

My Conceptual Framework

I will first describe how the three key concepts of my approach—fallibility, reflexivity, and the human uncertainty principle—apply to the financial markets. First, fallibility.

Market prices of financial assets do not accurately reflect their fundamental value because they do not even aim to do so. Prices reflect market participants' expectations of future market prices. Moreover, market participants are subject to fallibility; consequently, their expectations about the discounted present value of future earnings flows are likely to diverge from reality. The divergence may range from the negligible to the significant. This is in direct contradiction of the efficient market hypothesis, which does not admit fallibility.

Second, reflexivity. Instead of playing a purely passive role in reflecting an underlying reality, financial markets also have an active role: they can affect the future earnings flows they are supposed to reflect. That is the point that behavioral economists have missed. Behavioral economics focuses on only half of the reflexive process—cognitive fallibility leading to the mispricing of assets—and does not concern itself with the effects that mispricing can have on the fundamentals.

There are various pathways by which the mispricing of financial assets can affect the so-called fundamentals. The most widely used are those that involve the use of leverage—both debt and equity leveraging. For instance, companies can improve their earnings per share by issuing shares at inflated prices—at least for a while. Markets may give the impression that they are always right, but the mechanism at work is very different from that implied by the prevailing paradigm; markets affect the fundamentals they are supposed to reflect.

Third, the human uncertainty principle turns what economic theory treats as timeless generalizations into a time-bound historical process. If agents act on the basis of their imperfect understanding, equilibrium is far from a universally and timelessly prevailing condition of financial markets. Markets may just as easily tend away from a putative equilibrium as toward it. Instead of universally and timelessly prevailing, equilibrium becomes an extreme condition in which subjective market expectations correspond to objective reality. Theoretically, such a correspondence could be brought about by either the cognitive or the manipulative function by itself—either perceptions can change to match reality, or perceptions can lead to actions that change reality to match perceptions. But in practice, such a correspondence is more likely to be the product of a reflexive interaction between the two functions. Whereas traditional economics views equilibrium as the normal—indeed, necessary—state of affairs, I view such periods of stability as exceptional; rather, I focus on the reflexive feedback loops that characterize financial markets and cause them to be constantly changing.

Negative versus Positive Feedback Loops

Reflexive feedback loops can be either negative or positive. Negative feedback brings the participants' views and the actual situation closer together; positive feedback drives them further apart. In other words, a negative feedback process is self-correcting. It can go on forever, and if there are no significant changes in external reality, it may eventually lead to an equilibrium in which the participants' views come to correspond to the actual outcome.

That is what rational expectations theory expects to happen in financial markets. It postulates that there is a single correct set of expectations that people's views will converge around and that deviations are random—there is no built-in divergence between participants' forecasts and what comes to pass. That postulate has no resemblance to reality, but it is a core tenet of economics as it is currently taught in universities and even used in the models of central banks. In practice, market participants' expectations diverge from reality to a greater or lesser extent, and their errors may be correlated and significantly biased. That is the generic cause of price distortions. So equilibrium, which is the central case in mainstream economic theory, turns out to be an extreme case of negative feedback, a limiting case in my conceptual framework. Since equilibrium is so extreme that it is unlikely to prevail in reality, I prefer to speak of near-equilibrium conditions.

By contrast, a positive feedback process is self-reinforcing. It cannot go on forever because eventually the participants' views would become so far removed from reality that the participants would have to recognize them as unrealistic. Nor can the iterative process occur without any change in the actual state of affairs because positive feedback reinforces whatever tendency prevails in the real world. Instead of equilibrium, we are faced with a dynamic disequilibrium, or what may be described as far-from-equilibrium conditions.

There are myriad feedback loops at work in financial markets at any point in time. Some of them are positive, others negative. As long as they are more or less in balance, they cancel out each other and market fluctuations do not have a definite direction. I compare these swings to the waves sloshing around in a swimming pool as opposed to the tides and currents that may prevail when positive feedbacks preponderate. Since positive feedbacks are self-reinforcing, occasionally they may become so big that they overshadow all other tendencies in the market.

Negative feedback loops tend to be more ubiquitous, but positive feedback loops are more interesting because they can cause big moves both in market prices and in the underlying fundamentals. A positive feedback process that runs its full course is initially self-reinforcing in one direction, but eventually it is liable to reach a climax or reversal point, after which it becomes self-reinforcing in the opposite direction. But positive feedback processes do not necessarily run their full course; they may be aborted at any time by negative feedbacks.

Boom–Bust Processes

Building on these ideas, I have developed a theory about boom–bust processes, or bubbles (Soros 1987, 2008). Every bubble has two components: an underlying trend that prevails in reality and a misconception relating to that trend (see Figure 4). A boom–bust process is set in motion when a trend and a misconception reinforce each other. The process is liable to be tested by negative feedbacks along the way, giving rise to climaxes that may or may not turn out to be genuine. If a trend is strong enough to survive the test, both the trend and the misconception will be further reinforced. Eventually, market expectations become so far removed from reality that people are forced to recognize that a misconception is involved. A twilight period ensues, during which doubts grow and more people lose faith, but the prevailing trend is sustained by inertia. As Chuck Prince, former head of Citigroup, said during the twilight of the super bubble that culminated in 2008: "As long as the music is playing, you've got to get up and dance. We're still dancing." Eventually, a point is reached when the trend is reversed; it then becomes self-reinforcing in the opposite direction. Boom–bust processes tend to be asymmetrical: booms are slow to develop and take a long time to become unsustainable; busts tend to be more abrupt due to forced liquidation of unsustainable positions and the asymmetries introduced by leverage.

The simplest case is a real estate boom. The trend that precipitates it is easy credit; the misconception is that the value of the collateral is independent of the availability of credit. As a matter of fact, the relationship is reflexive. When credit becomes cheaper and more easily available,

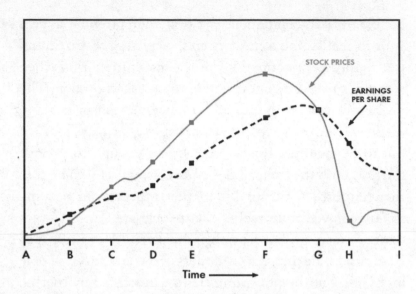

STOCK PRICES

EARNINGS
PER SHARE

A   B   C   D   E   F   G   H   I

Time ⟶

FIGURE 4. A typical market boom–bust. In the initial stage (AB),
a new positive earning trend is not yet recognized. Then comes
a period of acceleration (BC), when the trend is recognized and
reinforced by expectations. A period of testing may intervene,
when either earnings or expectations waiver (CD). If the
positive trend and bias survive the testing, both emerge stronger.
Conviction develops and is no longer shaken by a setback in
earnings (DE). The gap between expectations and reality becomes
wider (EF) until the moment of truth arrives when reality can
no longer sustain the exaggerated expectations and the bias is
recognized as such (F). A twilight period ensues, when people
continue to play the game although they no longer believe in
it (FG). Eventually, a crossover point (G) is reached when the
trend turns down and prices lose their last prop. This leads to a
catastrophic downward acceleration (GH), commonly known as
the crash. The pessimism becomes overdone, earnings stabilize, and
prices recover somewhat (HI).

activity picks up and real estate values rise. There are fewer defaults, credit performance improves, and lending standards are relaxed. So at the height of the boom, the amount of credit involved is at its maximum, and a reversal precipitates forced liquidation, depressing real estate values. Amazingly, the misconception continues to recur in various guises.

Other bubbles are based on different misconceptions. For instance, the international banking crisis of 1982 revolved around sovereign debt, in which case no collateral was involved. The creditworthiness of the sovereign borrowers was measured by various debt ratios, such as debt to GDP or debt service to exports. These ratios were considered objective criteria, but in fact, they were reflexive. When the recycling of petro-dollars in the 1970s increased the flow of credit to countries like Brazil, their debt ratios improved, which encouraged further inflows and started a bubble. In 1980, Paul Volcker raised interest rates in the United States to arrest inflation, and the sovereign debt bubble burst in 1982.

Bubbles are not the only form in which reflexivity manifests itself. They are just the most dramatic and the most directly contradictory to the efficient market hypothesis, so they deserve special attention. But reflexivity can take many other forms. In currency markets, for instance, the upside and downside are symmetrical so that there is no sign of an asymmetry between boom and bust. But there is no sign of equilibrium, either. Freely floating exchange rates tend to move in large, multiyear waves.

Markets versus Regulators

One of the most important and interesting reflexive interactions takes place between the financial authorities and the financial markets. Because markets do not tend toward equilibrium, they are prone to produce periodic crises. Financial crises lead to regulatory reforms. That is how central banking and the regulation of financial markets have evolved. Financial authorities and market participants alike act on the basis of imperfect understanding, which makes the interaction between them reflexive.

While bubbles occur only intermittently, the interplay between authorities and markets is an ongoing process. Misunderstandings by either side usually stay within reasonable bounds because market reactions provide useful feedback to the authorities, allowing them to correct their mistakes. But occasionally the mistakes prove to be self-validating, setting in motion vicious or virtuous circles. Such feedback loops resemble bubbles in the sense that they are initially self-reinforcing but eventually self-defeating; indeed, the intervention of the authorities to deal with periodic financial crises played a crucial role in the development of a super bubble that burst in 2007–2008 (Soros 2008, 2009). The interplay between markets and regulators is also at the heart of the euro crisis.

The Euro Crisis

I have been following the euro crisis closely ever since its inception. I have written numerous articles that have been collected in a book (Soros 2012). It would be impossible to summarize all my arguments for this essay; therefore, I shall focus only on the reflexive interaction between markets and authorities. Both acted on the basis of their imperfect understanding.

The design of the common currency had many flaws. Some of them were known at the time the euro was introduced. Everybody, for example, knew that it was an incomplete currency; it had a central bank, but it did not have a common treasury. The crash of 2008, however, revealed many other deficiencies. In retrospect, the most important was that by transferring the right to print money to an independent central bank, member countries ran the risk of default on their government bonds. In a developed country with its own currency, the risk of default is absent because it can always print money. But by ceding or transferring that right to an independent central bank, which no member state actually controls, the member states put themselves in the position of third-world countries that borrow in a foreign currency.

This fact was not recognized either by the markets or by the authorities prior to the crash of 2008, testifying to their fallibility. When the euro was introduced, the authorities actually declared government bonds to be riskless. Commercial banks were not required to set aside any capital reserves against their holdings of government bonds. The European Central Bank (ECB) accepted all government bonds on equal terms at the discount window. This set up a perverse incentive for commercial banks to buy the debt of the weaker governments in order to earn what eventually became just a few basis points because interest rates on government bonds converged to practically zero. This convergence in interest rates caused divergences in economic performance. The weaker countries enjoyed real estate and consumption booms, while Germany, which was dealing with the burden of reunification, had to adopt fiscal austerity and structural reforms.

After the Lehman bankruptcy, European finance ministers declared that no other systemically important financial institution would be allowed to fail; Chancellor Merkel then insisted that the obligation should fall on each country individually, not on the European Union or the Eurozone collectively. That was the onset of the euro crisis. It took markets more than a year to react to it. Only when Greece revealed a much larger than expected fiscal deficit did markets realize that Greece may actually default on its debt—and they raised risk premiums with a vengeance not only on Greek bonds but also on the bonds of all the heavily indebted member countries.

A Greek default would have created a worse banking crisis than the Lehman bankruptcy. The authorities put together a number of rescue packages, but they always did too little too late so conditions in Greece continued to deteriorate. This set a pattern for the other heavily indebted countries such as Spain, Italy, Portugal, and Ireland as well. While the actions of the ECB have calmed the markets, the crisis is still far from resolved. Rather than an association of equals, the Eurozone became divided into two classes: creditors and debtors. In a financial crisis, the creditors call the shots. The policies they are imposing perpetuate the division because the debtors have to pay risk premiums not only on government bonds but also on bank credit. The additional cost of credit, which is a recurrent burden, makes it practically impossible for the heavily indebted countries to regain competitiveness.

This is not the result of an evil plot. It was caused by a lack of understanding of an extremely complicated reality. In my articles, I put forward a series of practical proposals that could have worked at the time but became inadequate soon thereafter. Conversely, had the authorities adopted earlier some measures that they were willing to adopt later, they could have arrested the downtrend and then reversed it by adopting further measures. As it is, they have managed to calm the crisis but failed to reverse the trend.

This analysis emphasizes the vital role that fallibility plays in shaping the course of history: there would have been no crisis without it. It also shows that in far-from-equilibrium conditions, the normal rules do not apply. One of the reasons why the crisis persists is that the

Eurozone is governed by treaties that were designed for near-equilibrium conditions. Obviously, economists relying on the prevailing paradigm could not have reached this conclusion.

Toward a New Paradigm

One of the most powerful concepts for purposes of simplification is the concept of change. In my first philosophical essay (Soros 1962, 2006), written under the influence of Karl Popper, I used the concept of change to build models of social systems and reflexively connect them to modes of thinking. I linked organic society with the traditional mode of thinking, open society with the critical mode, and closed society with the dogmatic mode.

It can be seen that my conceptual framework extends to a much broader area than that covered by economic theory. But financial markets provide the best laboratory for studying far-from-equilibrium situations at work because they manifest themselves in fat tails that can be clearly observed in the data. They can be studied in other fields as well, but only in the form of a historical narrative, as I have done in my analysis of the euro crisis, which weaves together politics with financial economics.

Reflexivity has been largely neglected until recently because it connects different fields studied by different disciplines. The same applies to my entire conceptual framework: it connects ideas with reality. Reality has been broken up into narrow fields of specialization. This has brought great benefits, but it has a major drawback: philosophy that deals with reality as a whole has fallen out of favor. It needs to be rehabilitated.

Mainstream economics tried to seal itself off from reality by relying on postulates that turned out to be far removed from reality. The financial crisis of 2007–2008 and subsequent events exposed the weakness of this approach. The bankruptcy of Lehman Brothers was also the bankruptcy of the prevailing paradigm. There is urgent need for a new one.

This essay has shown that my interpretation of financial markets—based on my theory of reflexivity—is radically different from orthodox economics based on efficient markets and rational expectations. Strictly speaking, both interpretations are pseudo-scientific by Popper's standards. That is why I called my first book *The Alchemy of Finance*. And that is why some proponents of the efficient market hypothesis still defend it in the face of all the evidence.

Nevertheless, I contend that my interpretation yields better explanations and predictions than the prevailing paradigm. How can I reconcile this claim with my starting contention that the future is inherently uncertain and financial markets are inherently unpredictable? By resorting to Popper's logic of scientific discovery. As a market participant, I formulate conjectures and expose them to refutation. I also assume that other market participants are doing the same thing whether they realize it or not. Their expectations are usefully aggregated in market prices. I can therefore compare my own expectations with prevailing prices. When I see a divergence, I see a profit opportunity. The bigger the divergence, the bigger the opportunity. Popper made a similar assertion about scientific hypotheses. Philosophers of science roundly criticized him for this on the grounds that the predictive power of scientific theories cannot be quantified. It may not work for scientific theories, but I can testify from personal experience that it does work in the alchemy of financial markets.

When the price behavior contradicts my expectations, I have to reexamine my hypothesis. If I find myself proven wrong, I take a loss; if I conclude that the market is wrong, I increase my bet, always taking into account the risk that I am bound to be wrong some of the time. This works well in markets that are efficient in the sense that transaction costs are minimal; it does not work in private equity investments that are not readily marketable. My performance record bears this out. I was successful in markets but not in private equities. My approach can also be useful in formulating policy recommendations, as my articles on the euro crisis demonstrate.

CONCLUSION

Ever since the crash of 2008, there has been a widespread recognition, both among economists and the general public, that economic theory has failed. But there is no consensus on the causes and the extent of that failure.

I have argued that the failure is more profound than generally recognized. It goes back to the foundations of economic theory. Economics tried to model itself on Newtonian physics. It sought to establish universally and timelessly valid laws governing reality. But economics is a social science, and there is a fundamental difference between the natural and social sciences. Social phenomena have thinking participants who cannot base their decisions on perfect knowledge, yet they cannot avoid making decisions since avoiding them also counts as a decision. They introduce an element of indeterminacy into the course of human events that is absent in the behavior of inanimate objects. The resulting uncertainty hinders the social sciences in producing laws similar to Newton's physics. Yet once we recognize this difference, it frees us to develop new approaches to the study of social phenomena. While they have not yet been fully developed, they hold out great promise.

The stakes could not be higher. The mistaken theories that allowed the "super bubble" to build, the policy errors that were made in the wake of the crash, and the ongoing mishandling of the euro crisis highlight the human suffering that can result from a fundamental misunderstanding of the nature of economic systems. Recognizing the implications of our fallibility will be a great improvement in our understanding. Interpreting the economy as a reflexive system may not prevent future bubbles, crashes, or policy errors, but it may enable deeper insights into economic and sociopolitical phenomena and help humankind to better manage its affairs in the future.

I realize that my approach is still very rudimentary. For most of my life, I developed it in the privacy of my own mind. Only in recent years did I have the benefit of substantive criticism. It remains to be seen whether my conceptual framework can develop into a new paradigm. Much depends on whether reflexive feedback loops can be properly modeled. There is an obvious problem with modeling: Knightian uncertainty cannot be quantified. But it may be possible to identify trends without quantifying them and changes in trends without specifying the time of their occurrence. That is what I have done in my boom–bust model (Figure 4). We can also use volatility, which is quantifiable, as a substitute for uncertainty. And there may be other techniques that address these issues, such as Imperfect Knowledge Economics (Frydman and Goldberg 2013) or new approaches yet to be invented.

The new paradigm is bound to be very different from the one that failed. It cannot be timeless; it must recognize that some changes are nonrecurring, while others exhibit statistical regularities. Moreover, economic theory will not be able to seal itself off from other disciplines and from reality. There may be room for a series of paradigms linking economics with other disciplines like climate science.

Obviously, I shall not be able to develop these ideas due to my age. My creative years are nearly over. That is why I have established the Institute of New Economic Thinking (INET). I look to INET to build on the philosophical foundations I have outlined here.

REFERENCES

Beinhocker, Eric D. 2013. "Reflexivity, Complexity, and the Nature of Social Science." *Journal of Economic Methodology* 20, no. 4: 330–342.

Frydman, Roman, and Michael D. Goldberg. 2013. "The Imperfect Knowledge Imperative in Modern Macroeconomics and Finance Theory." In *Rethinking Expectations: The Way Forward for Macroeconomics*, edited by Roman Frydman and Edmund S. Phelps, 130–168. Princeton, NJ: Princeton University Press.

Keynes, John Maynard. 1936. *The General Theory of Employment, Interest, and Money.* New York: Harcourt Brace.

Knight, Frank H. 1921. *Risk, Uncertainty, and Profit.* Boston: Houghton Mifflin.

Mandelbrot, Benoît. 1963. "The Variation of Certain Speculative Prices." *Journal of Business* 36, no. 4: 394–419.

Merton, Robert K. 1949. *Social Theory and Social Structure.* New York: Free Press.

Popper, Karl. 1935/1959. *Logik der Forschung.* Vienna: Verlag von Julius Springer; *The Logic of Scientific Discovery.* London: Hutchinson.

———. 1944. "The Poverty of Historicism, II. A Criticism of Historicist Methods." *Economica* 11, no. 43: 119–137.

———. 1945. *The Open Society and Its Enemies.* London: Routledge.

———. 1957. *The Poverty of Historicism.* London: Routledge.

Robbins, Lionel. 1932. *An Essay on the Nature and Significance of Economic Science.* London: MacMillan.

Soros, George. 1962. *Burden of Consciousness.* Unpublished; revised version included in Soros 2006.

———. 1987. *The Alchemy of Finance.* Hoboken, NJ: Wiley & Sons.

———. 1998. *The Crisis of Global Capitalism: Open Society Endangered*. New York: PublicAffairs.

———. 2000. *Open Society: Reforming Global Capitalism*. New York: PublicAffairs.

———. 2006. *The Age of Fallibility: Consequences of the War on Terror*. New York: PublicAffairs.

———. 2008. *The New Paradigm for Financial Markets: The Credit Crisis and What It Means*. New York: PublicAffairs.

———. 2009. *The Crash of 2008 and What It Means: The New Paradigm for Financial Markets*. New York: PublicAffairs.

———. 2010. *The Soros Lectures at the Central European University*. New York: PublicAffairs.

———. 2012. *Financial Turmoil in the United States and Europe: Essays*. New York: PublicAffairs.

About the Author

 George Soros is founder and chair of Soros Fund Management LLC and the Open Society Foundations. Born in Budapest in 1930, he survived the Nazi occupation during World War II and fled Communist-dominated Hungary in 1947 for England, where he graduated from the London School of Economics. He then settled in the United States, where he accumulated a large fortune through the international investment fund he founded and managed.

Mr. Soros has been active as a philanthropist since 1979, when he began providing funds to help black students attend Cape Town University in apartheid South Africa. The Open Society Foundations today operate in more than one hundred countries, with annual expenditures of roughly $940 million, working to promote the values of open society, human rights, and transparency.

George Soros is the author of over a dozen books, including *The Tragedy of the European Union: Disintegration or Revival?* (2014). His articles and essays on politics, society, and economics regularly appear in major newspapers and magazines around the world.

PublicAffairs is a publishing house founded in 1997. It is a tribute to the standards, values, and flair of three persons who have served as mentors to countless reporters, writers, editors, and book people of all kinds, including me.

I. F. STONE, proprietor of *I. F. Stone's Weekly*, combined a commitment to the First Amendment with entrepreneurial zeal and reporting skill and became one of the great independent journalists in American history. At the age of eighty, Izzy published *The Trial of Socrates*, which was a national bestseller. He wrote the book after he taught himself ancient Greek.

BENJAMIN C. BRADLEE was for nearly thirty years the charismatic editorial leader of *The Washington Post*. It was Ben who gave the *Post* the range and courage to pursue such historic issues as Watergate. He supported his reporters with a tenacity that made them fearless and it is no accident that so many became authors of influential, best-selling books.

ROBERT L. BERNSTEIN, the chief executive of Random House for more than a quarter century, guided one of the nation's premier publishing houses. Bob was personally responsible for many books of political dissent and argument that challenged tyranny around the globe. He is also the founder and longtime chair of Human Rights Watch, one of the most respected human rights organizations in the world.

•   •   •

For fifty years, the banner of Public Affairs Press was carried by its owner Morris B. Schnapper, who published Gandhi, Nasser, Toynbee, Truman, and about 1,500 other authors. In 1983, Schnapper was described by *The Washington Post* as "a redoubtable gadfly." His legacy will endure in the books to come.

Peter Osnos, *Founder*

3119202179465